My

Tales fron

Sus

The Crossing Press
Freedom, CA 95019

Illustrations by Claudia McGehee
Cover & book design by Sheryl Karas

Printed in the U.S.A.

Library of Congress Cataloging-in-Publication Data

Baumgartner, Susan.
    My Walden : Tales from Dead Cow Gulch / by Susan Baumgartner;
illustrations by Claudia McGehee
             p. cm.
  ISBN 0-89594-552-5
  1. Solitude.   2. Simplicity.   3. Country life—Idaho.
4. Baumgartner, Susan.   I. Title.
BJ1499.S6B38 1992
818'.5403—dc20
[B]
                            92-2257
                              CIP

For Marilyn

Because she was the first to believe.
Because she never stopped believing.

Contents

STARS

I look around the cabin. It's 4:17 p.m., and already it's getting dark. Soon I'll have to light the candles to see anything at all, and when I can't stand that flickering dimness anymore, I'll have to resign myself to the hissing roar of the propane lantern. Stupid to start an adventure in January in northern Idaho.

Only two weeks into my stay here at Dead Cow Gulch, I don't want to admit to myself that I've made a mistake. But the darkness is really getting to me. There is no real light in the cabin until after 7:00 in the morning. It is already getting dark only nine hours later. Now, except for maybe one anxious, flashlight-toting trip to the outhouse, I'm stuck inside until morning. The cabin seems especially small with black night pushing in against all the windows. There was no dark in Seattle or Hartford or Syracuse. Ever. Having electricity seemed like a God-given right, as natural as having air to breathe, and even if I turned out my own lights, there was always that reflected glow of the city.

4:23 p.m. Getting darker. I'm fighting claustrophobia. I can't spend another endless evening trapped in here, going to bed at 8:00 to hide in the more familiar darkness behind my closed eyes. I think about those "take back the night" vigils, people with

1

candles banding together in a symbolic confrontation with fear and the dark.

Take back the night, Susan. Take it back.

I'm outside in an instant, zipping my coat as I go, sliding down the ramp that serves for front steps. I walk past the cabin, jump the narrow part of the creek and go on to the shelf of rock that juts out over the canyon. I stand there. If all I have in my world right now is dark, then I'm going to experience the full black darkness of it.

After a while I sit down on a low, weathered stump. I'm trying to figure the minimum time I have to endure out here on this adventure before I can surrender, and still retain at least some pride. If only I hadn't bragged about it to so many of my friends. I'm looking so hard inside, I don't pay much attention to the outside, all those hundreds of pine trees marching down the sides of the canyon, the blank of the sky overhead. In college, when things got rough, I always felt I had to tough it out at least through the semester. But that would mean spending over three more long months here. I'm not even sure I can get through this first one. I'm not even sure I can get through tonight.

Something makes me look up. Oh. That.

Starlight. Star bright. First star I see tonight.

I look away. Wishing on stars is dangerous. Sometimes you get what you think you want. Besides, it's probably not even a star. That first bright one is usually Venus.

Maybe two months out here would be long enough under the circumstances.

Again, something makes me look up. Another star. This one is so tiny and delicate, it must be a star, not a planet. And yet the sky still seems light. Certainly it's not the inky black I've always associated with night. I watch more closely. I remember something I read once when I was a kid, that the stars are always

there, that if you go way down inside a deep well on a sunny day and look up, you can see them. I always wanted to try that. And while I'm thinking about this, a third star appears. I stake out a blank patch of sky. I watch it closely. I blink, and when I look again a fourth star is just barely visible, so faint I wouldn't have noticed it unless I'd been looking.

I sit quietly and watch, so high above the canyon I feel closer to the sky than to the earth. It's as if the sun is drawing the light out of the sky as it sets, and as the curtain of light is pulled aside, the stars are revealed. Soon there are far more than I can count. The faint ones get brighter. More and more dim ones come into view. I stay until I lose all track of them. I stay until my legs go to sleep, finding out how the night happens.

Slowly, I get to my feet and look around. I'm way out here on the edge of the canyon without my flashlight and not even a candle lit in the cabin to guide me back. But it's not actually dark. There's a definite line between earth and sky. The black of branches is different from the black of trunks. The glow of starlight in the sky suffuses the patches of snow, brightens the ice in the creek. The cabin looms as a smoother shape against the rough darkness of the field. I walk slowly back, open the door and walk inside. And even here, it's not completely dark, not that kind of dark I was afraid of. As I reach for the candles, it occurs to me that I might just make it. I'm going to get through this first month anyway.

THOREAU

Henry David? Or David Henry? Thoreau with the accent on the second syllable or Thoreau pronounced like "thorough?" Either way, this man, Henry David Thoreau, has shaped my life. It was spring of 1973. I was a senior at the University of Idaho in Moscow. As usual, Idaho was a little behind the times and most of us were still living as if it were 1968, the height of the tumultuous sixties. Everything conspired against me—my youth, my idealism, and the times themselves. Innocently enough, I signed up for a class on Emerson, Thoreau and Whitman. Emerson was too cerebral. Whitman was too much. But Thoreau. The man got to me right away.

Each thing he said, I believed immediately and knew that I had always believed it. He spoke in illuminations. He uttered truths so obvious they were irrefutable. "I would rather sit on a pumpkin and have it all to myself than be crowded on a velvet cushion." Well, of course. A pumpkin was good and honest and unpretentious. And I was the oldest of eight children. Solitude was this precious thing, rarely experienced. A room of one's own was out of the question, but one might just manage a solitary pumpkin. "The mass of men lead lives of quiet desperation." Exactly. Just like all the adults around me who had squandered their lives grubbing for money and were now too old to do anything important, anything that really mattered. "I went to the woods because I wished to live deliberately, to front only the essential facts of life, and see if I could not learn what it had to teach, and not, when I came to die, discover that I had not lived." Yes. The shape of my life revealed to me in one profound sentence.

So I became a disciple of Thoreau. Degree in hand, all my possessions packed inside a single blue metal footlocker, I spent the summer of 1973 on the Oregon coast, scrubbing toilets at the Surftides Beach Resort for money, spending all my free time reading and walking beside the ocean and thinking and living simply. Except for the toilets, it was perfection.

After two semester's worth of a real job in Seattle, I spent the summer of 1974 working on the family farm near Genesee. I lived with my sister in our grandparents' old, old house called the Carlson Place, which is just a little over a mile from where I am now, last outpost on the gravel road to nowhere. There, I started my first novel and took long walks in the canyon and was ready to stay forever. But Thoreau had neglected to mention that it is helpful to be an heir to a pencil factory or to have one of America's leading philosophers as your patron. Having no such buttresses against reality, I was forced back into the labor pool.

I'd learned to type way back in high school, and that seemed to be the only skill I possessed that had any value in the real world. Everywhere I went I was a secretary and I hated that "quiet desperation" and I knew that my life was passing by without being lived. Moscow, Idaho. Bellingham, Washington. Petersburg, Alaska.

And then in the spring of 1980, I accidentally read some Thoreau again. Immediately, my secretarial life was unbearable. I saved my paychecks and wheedled and pleaded and managed to spend eight more precious months at the Carlson Place before the money ran out. Again I longed to stay forever, but I had to go back to being a secretary. Moscow, again. Then Hartford, Connecticut.

Still miserable, still trying to find a less desperate way to live, I was haunted once again by Henry David. In the fall of 1982, I visited Massachusetts and Walden. I was a little disappointed. In my mind, as I read Thoreau's words, Walden had been this vast wilderness. I was stunned to find only a thin strip of woods and the intrusion of an apartment complex on the bluff above. Even when I tried to visualize the place as it had been for Thoreau, it still seemed far too close to Concord for true solitude. If Thoreau could find such wildness in such a civilized place, how much more could I discover in the true wilderness of Idaho? In that moment, my future crystallized. Disdaining the noisy crowds of the designated swimming area, I walked clear around Walden Pond to the most solitary section and waded in. The act was illegal—"civil disobedience"—a sort of baptism.

Somehow I convinced my long-suffering parents to let me come back once more to Idaho. The Carlson Place was occupied, so this time it was the tiny bunkhouse hauled out to Dead Cow Gulch. I was secretly proud that my cabin at 9 by 12 feet was even smaller than Thoreau's 10 by 15 foot hermitage. No electricity this time, no indoor plumbing, no car. Pounding out pages and pages of novels every day on the ancient manual typewriter. It was tough, but it was also wonderful. I got to stay for almost a whole year, from January through December of 1983, but then, as usual, the money was gone.

A secretary, again. Moscow, again. Desperation. Depression. Despair. Maybe Thoreau was wrong. Maybe he had tricked me into living a miserable, unfulfilled, poverty-stricken life. So I turned my back on him. Graduate school. A job as a technical writer in New York. Suddenly I was making $26,000.00 a year, when I had never before earned more than $10,000.00. I bought a car and a VCR and an answering machine. I got a microwave oven. I wallowed in yuppie wealth. After three years of this I was deeply enmeshed in Corporate America. I was working ten hour days and weekends. But I'd also started writing for myself again, and it wasn't long before Thoreau insinuated himself back into my life. Once more I'd allowed myself to fall from the path of awareness and contemplation. My life was slipping by unnoticed.

Back to Idaho one more time in June of 1989. Back to the tiny cabin. But this time with a car and a half-time job. Compromise. Three and a half days in the real world making real money. Three and a half days out on Dead Cow Gulch in Thoreau's world living life.

Who knows what will happen next. Will I ever recover from that 1973 revelation when I felt Thoreau's truth in my soul and knew precisely what life should be? Will I continue to let this 19th century male dictate the shape of my life? Am I doomed to live this solitary existence in pursuit of a lifestyle that is no longer possible? I don't know. I suppose that is what makes it interesting, this ongoing battle between the real world and the world I want to exist. I would probably be miserable being ordinary. I would miss being a rebel. After all these years I've embraced the same kind of perversity that made Thoreau such an irritating and yet intriguing person. So I guess I'll keep doing what all of us Thoreauvian disciples do—retire to the woods to live in a cabin and then bore everyone by writing about it.

BROWN

feel grey today. No, I don't. I feel brown. Grey is a magical color—grey with an "e," never gray with an "a." Grey is all about moors and Merlin and druids and Celts. Grey is the color of fantasy novels and London mornings. Grey is all about the world of elves where anything can happen around the next mist-shrouded bend.

So I feel brown. Brown is late February when it hasn't snowed for a while and the few patches of snow that are left have turned glacier-like and dirty. The sky is dark with clouds. Inside the cabin, it is brown. Nothing comes through the skylight. In fact, the words "sky" and "light" seem like antonyms, the skylight a ridiculous architectural construct that mocks its intended purpose. Outside, the bare fields all around on both sides of the canyon are brown, smooth brown of seeded winter wheat, rough brown of stubble plowed ground. The grass around the cabin is dead and brown. The trees seem tired and cold. The air is frozen dry. The world itself is like a dry stone, muted and uninteresting. It needs moisture, it needs dipping into a stream, to shine and show its true colors. So I am brown today, brown down into my soul.

Time for a walk. Just get out of here. Usually I take the high road, the deer trail around the edge of the alfalfa field. It helps to

9

see the openness of the sky, even though the sky today, as it has been for the past many days, is heavy and close with clouds. But something draws me down the logging road into the canyon. I know this is dangerous. I'll feel more trapped than ever down here with all the trees closing in around me. The barren open field would be less barren than the sight of this usually wild and lively place frozen into waiting. But I keep walking anyway. I'm too brown to do anything logical like turn around and climb up out of this hole.

Suddenly there's a staccato pounding just ahead. I still my heavy footsteps on the frozen road. Woodpecker? Yes. The sound is loud in the silenced woods. I creep closer. I'm looking for the woodpeckers I usually see around here, the little grey and beige mottled ones with the black crescent, like an ascot, at their throats. They have two tiny patches of coral-colored feathers on either side of their faces, and when they fly, they reveal that same coral shade, solid, under their wings. I always watch long enough to see them fly.

But this woodpecker, too intent on his noisy hammering to notice me right away, is the traditional kind of woodpecker, the "Woody the Woodpecker" kind. He's shiny black and vivid red and starkly white. I've hardly ever seen his kind here in the canyon, and never this close. His colors are so bright even the air around him seems brighter during those few moments before he finally senses my presence and streaks away, peeved at being interrupted.

I walk on. The forest is quiet again. I sink back into brownness. The road is too familiar. I'm seeing what I always see down here, only less. Maybe if there could be smells. I want dampness and the smell of moss and the spicy aroma of pine. At least the dreary walk is almost over. Soon I'll reach the big clearing and it'll be time to turn back.

Then to my left I see a great tangled burst of color. It's not purple. It's not lavender. It's some color in between, a lavender more intense than any lavender has ever been allowed to be. What is it? All the other foliage is brown against the backdrop of drab evergreen trees that have been green too long without renewal. I move closer. I see tangled vines thick with thorns. I try to get my bearings. This is the same place I visited so often in summers past, watching and waiting, sampling and shuddering and waiting some more. Blackcap bushes? Has to be. I never dreamed the canes would turn such a gorgeous shade of purple. In summer they looked kind of greenish-brown and ordinary, covered with leaves and the tiny little berries that truly must be black to be eaten.

Surprised, I walk on to the clearing and turn around. On my return, I try to sneak up on the spiny canes, convinced they will have reverted to a normal color, but they are just as vibrantly lavender as before. The color still seems impossible, the kind of storybook bright thorns the Brothers Grimm would likely plant around Sleeping Beauty's castle, but I must accept the testimony of my own eyes.

Walking on, I feel less brown, maybe only tan now, moving into taupe. I'll go back to the cabin, read a trash novel, eat chocolate, slob out. Decadence, giving in, is sometimes a better cure than virtuous productivity. I move around a wide switchback, hemmed in by trees. Then up a small rise and suddenly there is a little break in the trees to the north like a scenic overlook on a mountain road. At first I can't recognize what I'm seeing. A thin band of color has been stamped onto the top of Moscow Mountain. It is the sky. It is a small patch of sky without clouds, the sky with sun touching it. It is blue. I'd forgotten blue. I'd forgotten *this* blue, crystalline, deepening with the early afternoon setting of the sun. I stay to watch it until the clouds sink slowly down to touch the mountain and hide the sky from my sight.

I walk again, folding my arms over my chest to hold the colors in. I saw red. I saw purple. I saw blue. Color still exists. Knowing that, it's worth hanging on here until spring.

SOLITAIRE

I play solitaire. Usually during that last dim half hour of candlelight just before I can't stand it anymore and start the propane lantern. Why? Because the long, dark evenings make me sad. Because I can't see to do anything else. Because it seems so frivolous.

When I play solitaire, I cheat. I can't bear it when the game gets stuck and can't be finished. I like things to be finished, completed, nicely put away. But I do have very specific rules about the types of cheating I can do, and how long I have to be frustrated before I move a card to get the game going again. Solitaire gives me something to do. It's another tiny ritual to hold on to from one unstructured day to the next.

It is my first year at Dead Cow Gulch. I don't have a job and I don't have a car. I truly live here, my only escape for showers and companionship dependent on the kindness of family and friends. Solitaire is the only game I play.

It's been seven days, eight, maybe nine since I've seen a human face or heard someone speak. I walked out this morning, Thursday, to check the box we've set up at the Carlson Place where traveling family members are supposed to leave my mail, but no one was there and the mail was meager, not even the usual Wednesday *Time* magazine. I left a pitiful note: Must get out. Saturday morning. 7:00 a.m. If you happen to be driving to town.

What to do in the meantime. Okay, another long walk around the edge of the alfalfa field. I talk to myself, making up conversations. Maybe one more mile, to use up time, so I'll be real tired, so I can go to bed early tonight. Back at the cabin. Another list. All the things I planned to do here. All the things I could do if only I had money. All the improvements I would make. All the life pleasures I would buy. Hundreds of candles. Electricity. A car. I pace inside the cabin, twitchy, restless, depressed, weepy. Then pages and pages and pages in my journal. Why did I want this? What made me come here?

Out in the real world, I craved solitude. Life moved too fast. There were too many interruptions. I was unconscious most of the time, barely aware of what I was doing or why. And people were hard for me, had always been hard. How to talk to them. How to read what they were thinking. How to do those social things that seemed natural for anyone else but hopelessly contrived when I attempted them. Shy. A loner. A dreamer. Happier in my own world than in theirs.

But here in the cabin, after eight days, the aloneness is becoming loneliness. It seems impossible that I could ever have wanted to get away from people. No chance though of escaping until Saturday morning, and even then, the ride is not for sure. Maybe nobody's coming down that day. Maybe no one's planning to go up to the home farm near Genesee. It would take a long time to walk the seventeen miles into town.

I can't bear it. My isolation becomes a crucible. I burn in loneliness all Thursday night and all day Friday. It is 5:00 p.m. Still fourteen hours until I will know my fate—escape at last or more days alone. I demand that there be solace, but there is none. I insist that my fate is unbearable, unendurable, but no one relents. I wanted this, I have chosen this, and now it will destroy me. Before I feared sliding through life unconscious. Now I am too conscious, aware of every long moment that passes. I start to cry. I shout up at the darkening sky. I plead for mercy. No one hears me. No one is moved.

The next day—escape. I am joyous as I settle on the filthy seat of the old pickup truck, stumbling over words to try to express the feeling of relief. My tongue is stiff. My throat aches from the effort of articulating all these syllables. I've lost the pattern and the pace of conversation. I am like a wild thing, easily flustered amidst the frenzied activity of quiet little Idaho towns. Everything is a wonder to me—the people, the stimulation, water that comes out of faucets, lights that just turn on.

I stretch the time in civilization, two days, three, four, but inevitably I have to go back. I am afraid. And the loneliness waits. It is there as soon as I open the cabin door. It is like a great rock and I am dashed against it, over and over, week after week, until finally the constant pounding makes me strong. Then I stand up and face the loneliness and we prepare to do battle. Out here we play solitaire for keeps.

NAMES

My home town of Genesee. Named, perhaps, after the town and the river in up-state New York. Troy. Named for the city in Greece. Princeton. Harvard. Vassar. Obvious origins. Delusions of grandeur in a frontier territory. Lewiston and Clarkston. Christened to honor the two famous explorers who passed through them. Potlatch. Named for the extravagant gift exchanges between North Pacific Coast Indian tribes. Pullman, across the state line in Washington. Changed from Three Forks in the hope of getting the railroad to come through. Moscow. Final, geopolitically bizarre, name choice following appellations like Paradise, Hog Heaven and Taxthinma —the place of the mule deer fawns. Palouse. For Pelluts, the name the Nimipu, the "real people," the Nez Perce Indians gave to the river and this region that it flows through, so that now we are the Pelluts-pu, the people of the Palouse. Idaho. From the Shoshone word, E-dah-how, that means "Behold the sun coming down from the mountains." Or so the myth proclaims it.

It is early March. I have settled in a bit, gotten past the first traumas of how to start fires and how to boil my contacts and how to find water. I finally have time to go out exploring today, not far, just around the cabin and the creek and across the little land bridges to the other side. The snow from the last blizzard is

almost gone. I shuffle through the long brown grass.

What is that gleam of white over there? I nudge at it with the toe of my boot. A rib bone. A big one. How did that get here? Then other bones, leg bones and vertebrae and big knuckly knee bones and, when I'm least expecting it, a complete skull. It begins to seem too macabre. I'm living in a bone field.

I ask about it. Dad says that in the olden days there were several land bridges across this part of the creek. Grazing cows would simply wander back and forth, heedless of the little trickle of water that flowed like a subterranean spirit far below them. But back then the fields weren't tiled and the spring run-off was wildly uncontrolled. The creek would swell all at once, the sudden surge of water working against the underside of the solid-looking span, and the weight of a cow was enough to send everything, dirt and sod and bovine beast into the raging torrent.

The bones I have been finding are cow bones, the bones of animals drowned and washed ashore years ago. It seems awful in a way that I have chosen to begin my quest for meaning in this place of death. I had thought of christening my new home with a beautiful name, an inspirational name, ShangriLa or Camelot or Lothlórien or Arcadia. But over time, a new name begins to grow on me. Something with bones. Something with cows. Something about a tiny stream that can suddenly become monstrous. And then one day when I stumble across another skull buried in the grass, it comes to me. Dead Cow Gulch. The name sounds right. It says frontier and wild west, rough-hewn and countrified. It's slightly humorous and yet slightly menacing, a touch of grit to cut the sticky sweetness of my idealistic ways, the provincial ingenuousness I can't seem to outgrow no matter how many dark, foreign films I see. It's a name that fits the place. Dead Cow Gulch.

Friends with a sense of humor send letters to the Genesee address where I get my mail, but enclose inside envelopes with an address of Hermit House Number One, Dead Cow Gulch, Idaho 83000. The community is small, population one. The infrastructure, never built, has little chance of crumbling. The ghosts, so far as I know, are bovine, lowing plaintively just below hearing. In spite of its morbid history, it is a pleasant enough spot, a good neighborhood, a nice place to live.

DAILY BREAD

Most people believe that there are four major food groups. But out here at Chez Gulch there are only three— casseroles and sandwiches and chocolate. In fact, someday I'm going to write "The Chocolate Sandwich Casserole Cookbook," and live off the royalties for the rest of my life.

I am embarrassed about my eating habits. Living this pure existence, I know I should be consuming locusts and honey, wheat germ and tofu, alfalfa sprouts and yogurt. Or I should be living off the land.

But I don't. I think it's perversity, but out here I crave junk food. I dream, sometimes, of French fries. I fantasize that Yahweh will have an off day, get confused, and sow M & M's in my wilderness. My body cries out for cholesterol.

That is why I've settled on my three food groups. Casseroles are for breakfast. It's important to have a good breakfast. I know that. But I don't like cereal, hot or cold, and eggs or pancakes are too hard to fix in the morning when I'm not really awake yet. Much better to have stuff like that once in a while for dinner, the last meal of the day that true Idahoans call "supper." Once I did one of those diets where you eat breakfast and lunch, but have those grainy "milkshakes" for dinner. I got so tired of missing the main meal every day that I started having my main meal for breakfast. The diet ended rather quickly, as most diets do, but the backwards eating schedule has become a tradition.

There are lots of wonderful things to have for breakfast, things almost worth getting out of bed for. Lasagne. Tuna noodles. Spaghetti. Cold pizza. Shipwreck casserole. Chicken enchiladas. Stew. Dublin Coddle. A bulgur wheat-rice-barley dish I call "glop." Chili. Chow mein.

Hearty breakfasts make you tough. If you can get through a bowl of chili at 6:30 in the morning, you can get through anything else that happens to come along during the day. Maybe that's why most Americans are such wimps, creeping around all morning on a bit of fruit or a scrap of dry toast.

Cooking is not easy out here. There's a two burner propane camp stove. The refrigerator is an ice chest that lives under the northeast corner of the house. It's buried in a deep hole with only the lid above ground. Along the bottom beam of the cabin there, I've nailed a doubled gunny sack which hangs down to help keep that corner in the shade. In the summer, I bring out those blue freezer packs, but in spite of all my precautions, the food still sometimes spoils. Green eggs and ham can be a reality out here. Usually, I make the casseroles in bulk at the civilized home farm, then divide them into single portions and freeze them. I haul out just enough servings for the days I'll be here, and then heat one up each morning.

Sandwiches are for lunch. Sometimes I have hot dogs or make BLT's. A special favorite is bagel, fake lox (I can't, alas, get real lox in Idaho) and cream cheese. There are precise rules for sandwiches. Tuna or ham sandwiches must have potato chips layered inside. Chicken sandwiches should not. Roast beef sandwiches should have mustard. Meatloaf sandwiches should not. Salmon sandwiches should have just a touch of dill. Smoked turkey sandwiches should have a tiny bit of slivered onion. Almost all sandwiches should have lots of lettuce.

This is how I make my most favorite sandwich of all. First I have to go outside, down the ramp and around to the "fridge." Crouching down, I lift the gunny sack and hook it out of the way. Then I open the door of the ice chest and lean it back against the floor joist so it doesn't fall shut again. I hope. I take out bread, a small container of mayonnaise, small container of mustard, hunk of cheese, hunk of summer sausage, a cucumber and a head of lettuce. Balancing all this stuff along my left arm, I try to hold it there with my fingers, while I use my right hand to close the lid. I climb the ramp again, navigate through the screen door and the door without dropping anything, and sort of cascade everything onto the desk.

The desk is the heart of the cabin. It *is* a desk. It's also an "island" of the "kitchen" and the dining room table and the place where I keep everything from silverware to postage stamps and the platform I climb up on so I can make the bed.

I get out the breadboard and start the ritual of putting together this best sandwich I've ever invented. It must have all the proper ingredients placed in exactly the right order for it to be perfect. Dark and Grainy Less bread. Best Foods (Hellmann's) light mayonnaise. Grey Poupon mustard. Summer sausage, home-made, if possible. Cheddar cheese. Four to six 3/4 inch thick cucumber slices. Potato chips, preferably Blue Bell Riplets dip chips. Lots of lettuce. My friends know this as the bread-mayon-naise-mustard-summer sausage-cheese-cucumber-potato chip-lettuce-mustard-mayonnaise-bread sandwich. It is sublime.

Chocolate is for as often as necessary. Chocolate is focus when I'm having trouble writing. Chocolate is energy on a slow day. Chocolate is bribery when I have too much work to do. Chocolate is solace. Chocolate is celebration. Chocolate is the ultimate pleasure, especially when combined with reading. Chocolate is sex when nothing else is available. Chocolate is the worst addiction I have, and one I fight to overcome, usually to no avail.

Dinner/supper is light—an apple, cheese and crackers, some string beans, soup. It's too hard to cook at night, and I know I'll be getting up to something hot and nourishing in the morning.

Someday, soon, I'll convert to all the healthy stuff. I'll renounce my protein heritage and go vegetarian. I'll get off chocolate. I'll become lithe and translucent and ephemeral, a true spirit of the outdoors. But until I get around to doing that, I'm having one hell of a gastronomically good time.

MIDDLE GROUND I

I live on the middle ground. These 8.6 acres at the edge of the canyon used to be an alfalfa field, the far northeastern outpost of a farming empire. Before that, this was a wheat field. The slope was steep and nothing stood between the sharper decline of the canyon proper and the heavily laden grain trucks but a low, barbed wire fence. Many's the time a truck went sliding on the slick golden straw toward the abyss, only to be stopped at the last moment. Hay trucks fared little better.

Finally the farmers surrendered to the topography. In 1980, they turned their backs on the precept that agriculture must extend over every square foot of arable soil. They left the alfalfa patch to grow wild.

The cabin sits on the lower, southern end of this sloping bench. Originally, it was supposed to go on up the hill to the north, but January ice defeated the big truck and trailer, and we slid the cabin off here, as far as we could get it.

Often I climb that hill, still basking in the sun when the cabin has long been in the shade. I look out over the canyon, rank upon rank of pines processing down into the river-worn floor like dark cowled monks on their way to Vespers. Savoring the Benedictine look of the trees, I regret that the cabin isn't up here, that it rests instead in the little hollow below me. But when the winter wind scours the hilltop, I am grateful for my protected draw. And at the height of summer, when there is more than enough baking sun, I'm grateful for the early shade.

To the south and the west, my home is bordered by wheat fields. Or barley fields. Or pea fields on alternate years. The fields are rural, and yet they are part of civilization. Spray planes spread fertilizer and insecticides. Big, noisy tractors work the soil and fertilize it some more and seed it and work it again in the fall. Combines, like huge lawn mowers, circle relentlessly, cutting the peas or grain, thrashing it, augering out the harvest into waiting trucks. It is corporate agriculture—big fields, big machines, big yields and big bills for chemicals. The farmers, trapped now in this cycle of bigness, are just as poor as they've always been.

To the north and the east lies the canyon. It is hardly an old growth forest. They log down there. They cut firewood. They run cattle. It has logging roads and fences. Still, compared to the surrounding land, the canyon is wilderness. Wild creatures try to live wild there in spite of frequent human interruptions. The deer and elk and coyotes and hawks and owls and chipmunks have learned to live around my own intrusions and the infestations of loggers and three-wheelers and hunters.

But I live in the middle ground. I am not fully a part of the civilized world to the west. I am not fully a part of the wild world to the east. I live somewhere, uneasily, between both worlds, not sure yet where I truly belong. That is why I am here in this abandoned alfalfa field, caught between, testing both worlds, waiting to find out.

SLUGS

Nightmare. I hope. I huddle in the bunk bed with my blankets over my head, afraid to see if the nightmare is true. Slugs. There are slugs everywhere. They're pressed against the windows of the cabin, drooling slug slime down the panes. They've climbed onto the roof and completely covered the skylight so the morning sun can't penetrate. They push everywhere against the timbers of the cabin trying to ooze through and get me. I'm imprisoned inside, armed with a small Kerr jar full of salt, determined to defend myself.

I know why this is happening. It started yesterday. I had an attack of cabin fever and kind of went berserk. Winter is over, I guess. It's been raining and raining and raining for days. Even when the rain stops, it's still overcast and damp. I'm sick of it. I'm sick of getting wet every time I go outside. I'm sick of the mud. And I'm especially sick of the slugs. I should be grateful, I know. They're not the huge and hideous khaki green slugs of Washington and Oregon. They're not the even huger and more hideous banana slugs with their mustard yellow bodies and black spots. They're just little Idaho slugs, dark brown or black, not even an inch long, living a precarious existence in a dry land.

But there are so many of them and they are everywhere. I can't walk down the ramp without stepping on them. I open the

outhouse door and they're snuggled in lines between the bottom of the door and the platform. They're all over the wood in the woodpile. I have to check each piece before I carry it in to the stove. Two days ago there was a slug on the stick I use to clean the slugs off the firewood.

And yesterday morning I woke up, again, to the sound of rain on the skylight, monotonous and relentless. I got up in the grey light. It took me two tries to get the fire going because everything in the cabin is damp and the world has forgotten the dry heat of the sun. Then I went out to get stuff for breakfast. Slugs on the ramp. Slugs on the hanging gunny sack that shades the refrigeration system. And when I opened the ice chest, a slug nestled on my loaf of bread, happily generating slime in an attempt to eat through the plastic bag and have breakfast. My breakfast.

So I lost it. Too much. Too gross. I flicked the slug out with the stick and slammed the lid down and went into the house and got my jar of salt. I went crazy. I started on the ramp, spooning salt on the helpless little bodies, watching the slugs bubble and fizz as they disintegrated into pools of mucous. I salted everything within ten feet of the ice chest. I poured salt on little clumps of slugs huddled together along the base of the cabin. I went out into the old alfalfa field, the slugs just lying there by the hundreds.

And then I laughed at myself, this crazed woman out in the morning drizzle, waging futile chemical warfare against a horde of vicious gastropods. I put the lid back on the salt, now about half gone, and crept past the carnage into the cabin. I felt sheepish but a little better during the day. Nothing like throwing a cabin fever fit to ease tensions.

But now, today, I'm overcome by this guilty nightmare that's got me trapped in the bunk bed afraid to get up. Here I am, supposedly striving to be one with nature, just back from a serial slaughter of some of her children. I pull the blankets down. I open one eye. It's dark, but I can't tell if that's because the avenging slugs really have congregated over the skylight or simply because it's cloudy. Again.

I can believe in a slug attack. It's about time. The earth and the creatures of the earth put up with so much from us. I wonder sometimes if the plants and animals and elements won't eventually band together and fight back, try to drive us off the planet so they can set about healing the wounds accumulated through thousands of years of human abuse. It would serve us right if the earth, our mother, threw us out of the house.

I turn over and open both eyes. It's dark because it's cloudy. There's not a single slug on the skylight. I climb down the ladder. There are no slugs pushing against the windows. When I go outside for the first time, I step as carefully as I can down the ramp. Okay, slugs. Truce. It can't rain forever. We'll coexist somehow in this dampness. You stay out of my food. I'll try not to step on you. We'll share the land as best we can until the sun comes out again and you retreat back to your hidden homes in the moist places of the world while I inhabit the parts that are dry.

JEANS

Jeans. I love them. I wear them every day, all day, 365 days a year if I can get away with it. I am addicted to them. I'm living here at Dead Cow Gulch partly because the dress code is so informal and because jeans are almost a necessity for survival. But it wasn't always like this.

My first week as a freshman at the University of Idaho, I wore a dress every day because, at my high school, girls had been required to wear dresses. And yet I couldn't help noticing that almost all the other female students, at least the non-sorority ones, were wearing jeans.

My second week as a freshman at the University of Idaho, I wore jeans every day. The first time I slid into a desk wearing jeans was almost a religious experience. Denim against wood in a room that reeked of chalk dust. I felt natural, comfortable, exactly right.

The sixties finally came to Idaho in the early seventies, and we were changing the world. I knew it was only a matter of time before everyone, from the lowliest janitor to the president of the United States, would be wearing jeans and T-shirts. Those old, uncomfortable, impractical, sexist, establishment uniforms would be gone forever.

But the dream of the sixties died and I started buying panty hose again. I reached the ultimate level of "dress for success" as a technical writer for a computer graphics company in New York. Our little band of writers worked as part of the Marketing Department where image was everything. Red suspenders. The power tie. Three piece suits. I wore suits or dresses and high heels every day. There were difficulties—hiking the miles of corridors, crawling around on the floor behind computers trying to document the cabling system—but I never dreamed of wearing anything else.

Then, disaster, corporate shake-up. The tech writing department was merged with engineering. For a while, the five of us held out against that 50-member force of nerds and dweebs, swearing we would never be reduced to wearing corduroy pants and pocket protectors. I was the first to break. As the weeks rolled by and I became just another hacker hidden away in my cube, I started wearing low-heeled shoes, then nice slacks, and on one cold, dreary day, jeans. It was all downhill from there. I was a free woman. I could sit and move comfortably. I could jog down the halls for corporate emergencies. My jean addiction only got worse when I moved back to Idaho.

In fact, that addiction may be one of the driving forces behind my decision to try living at Dead Cow Gulch. Just because the rest of the world failed to adopt the egalitarian uniform of jeans and T-shirts, didn't mean that I had to give up my denim comfort.

My favorite pair of jeans right now is my oldest pair of jeans. They're faded whitish blue in places and they're incredibly soft. The waistband is just barely tight enough to keep the jeans from falling off when I stand up. For a while they had a small hole in the lower right thigh section. It seemed like all the arctic air of the earth would flow through that one, tiny opening. But Mom patched the hole, and the jeans were fine again, although better suited, perhaps, to summer weather. Now they should last at least another year, another year of comfort and durability and convenient pockets and freedom from fussing about my clothes.

Time to take a stroll through the canyon. I like looking down at myself as I walk, seeing the shape of my legs, taking pleasure in the way the jeans drape aesthetically over my sneakers. How could anything humans choose to wear be more attractive or cuter or say more about freedom than these tough but sexy denim pants from our frontier past? Nope. I refuse to change. It's up to everyone else. Not till the world goes back to wearing jeans, will I consider going back to the world.

CANIDS

Native Americans, as I understand it, often use a totem or an animal spirit to guide them. If I have a totem here, it is the coyote, brother to all the other canids of his genus, *Canis latrans, Canis lupus, Canis familiaris*.

Left to my own devices, I would never have dreamed of living like this. I was a wimp child, a house child, disdaining the physical. The outdoors, after all, is far too uncomfortable for reading. The ground is hard and lumpy. Bugs are everywhere. The wind ripples the pages. The light is too bright or too dim. Thoreau also provided the impetus, but over a period of years, it was Canids that made me brave enough to try this adventure in the woods.

Like many adolescents, devastated by the unanticipated discovery that humanity is far from perfect, I turned for comfort to animal companionship. Even on a farm, the range of choices was not that wide. I was afraid of the horses. Cows were out of the question. Chickens, even worse. Cats, no way. That left the family dog, a wild-haired black terrier mix, or any dog I happened to run into.

This experience pulled me a little from my own moody, self-absorption. Slowly it dawned on me that there were other ways of viewing the world. It became a challenge to try to see things through the eyes of another species. A few absent-minded strokes in search of solace became long periods of contemplation. Where do they really like to be scratched? Why? What do paws feel like? How do paws compare to hands? What is it that makes their eyes so especially beautiful? How can they sense all those different odors? Why is it such a delight for these creatures to smell so awful? What do these games of submission and dominance really mean to them?

I spent more time outside. I tried to look at the outdoors the way my new canid friends did. I celebrated their laziness, their curiosity, their fierceness, their exuberance, their goofiness. I spent hours just sitting, watching, sniffing, listening, snoozing, scratching, stretching, basking. The more time I spent with them, the more value I could see in the way they lived. It was still dirty and inconvenient outdoors, but also endlessly fascinating. I began to want to see if I had any chance of getting back some of what we humans had lost centuries before when we picked up a stick and spoke our first word and turned our backs on the animal world.

It is after 8:00 and the sun has just gone down. I'm doing the dishes. Then through the open windows I hear the first plaintive cry. I hurry outside, drying my hands on my denim-clad thighs. In moments, the cries are all around me, coyotes everywhere, one in the field behind me, a group down in the creek bed, a family just below the cabin. They howl, yelp, shriek. Single voices stand out and then weave themselves into the general wailing.

At first, old human fears tingle up my spine and chill the flesh at the back of my neck. But then I remember that these are sisters and brothers. I tip my head back. I listen carefully to catch the pitch. I join my voice with theirs. We are wonderful

together. We wail out our lonesomeness. We cry for the loss of the sun. We call to each other for reassurance. We sing our wildness. We prepare for the hunt. The voices rise around me, a shrill ululation that sends more chills down my back. A few of us give last wavering proclamations of our existence and then all is quiet. Regretfully I go inside to light the candles and finish the dishes and return to my human self.

I see the coyotes more in their sign than in the flesh. I see the four-leaved-clover-like tracks of their paws in the dust or the mud or the snow. I find their scat in quantity on the road. They seem never to tire of trying to tell the human interloper that this is their road, their territory, their place. Mostly we know of each other's presence and we sing together in the dark. That is enough for me. Canids first led me to discover the natural world and they stay with me here to help me find the wildness that still exists at the center of my being.

Perhaps I am romanticizing the coyotes and the other canids. Perhaps I am committing the usual human sin of demeaning our fellow creatures, projecting our own desires onto them, anthropomorphizing them, refusing to accept them for what they are. And yet I want the coyote to be my totem, my animal spirit. That is the reality of my species, making meaning from the things we see. And so I continue to watch for the coyotes. I take each canid visitation as a sign of blessing on my work here. I try to stay open to the messages they bring, one solitary human learning slowly to be less arrogant and more useful to the earth.

OUTHOUSES

O kay, we've put this off long enough. It's time to talk about outhouses.

The outhouse at Dead Cow Gulch is special because my grandfather built it. He made it with boards from an old barn that he tore down. In a few of the protected places you can still see a bit of the original red paint that isn't really red at all but kind of the maroon color of dried blood. It's the simplest possible construction, a wooden platform of two-by-fours, a half floor, the seat, plain board walls, a door on hinges and a tin roof. Add a hook on the outside to keep it closed, a hook on the inside for at least the illusion of privacy, and a spike toenailed in to hold the toilet paper. Center it over a hole, a big hole, and you're in business.

It's a nice outhouse, small, intimate, a single-seater. The wood of the seat is old and has been rubbed smooth over the years. It warms quickly, even in winter.

There are certain rules though that you have to follow when you are the proud owner of an outhouse:

1. Never close the door.
2. Never leave the toilet paper overnight.
3. Never wash the seat in winter.

Most people don't like outhouses because they don't know about rule number one. Make sure you live so far out in the dingtoolies that you rarely have to close the door. Closing the door can turn an otherwise perfectly pleasant outhouse into a dark fetid place to be visited for only the briefest periods when absolutely necessary.

The first thing then, that you must acquire, is a perfect outhouse door rock. The rock must be big enough to keep the door from swinging shut in the hardest winds, but small enough to nudge easily into place with your foot. I found mine by dangling head first over the creek that flows through Dead Cow Gulch and dredging up stones from the muck until I found one that was just right. So when I go out to the outhouse, I first wedge the door open and then make myself comfortable. From this sylvan seat I can see the cabin, all the trees around, the sky, and the dirt road that winds up through the fields. If there are visitors, they have to come down that road, and I'll see them long before they see me. Plenty of time to push the rock aside and pull the door shut.

Rule number two. When I make my final evening trip to the outhouse, I always bring the toilet paper back with me. Why? Because I have a furry neighbor who likes the taste of toilet paper or maybe just likes the fun of shredding it up. A dorm room or honeymoon car or office festooned with toilet paper is sort of funny. An outhouse toilet papered with your last roll when you live seventeen miles from town is seldom funny. Never leave the toilet paper overnight.

And rule number three. I made the mistake of washing down the outhouse only once. Froze solid. It took my posterior and me several days to thaw it out. I've found that the only equipment you really need to clean an outhouse is a broom. Just sweep it out once in a while, dirt from dust storms, cobwebs, dried mud from your boots. That's all it takes. No cleansers, no disinfectants, no deodorizers, no toilet brushes, no scrubbing under the rim. It's wonderful. I always hated cleaning the bathroom.

It's nice here. The boards in the walls have weathered and contracted and pulled apart. A fresh wind blows through. The early morning sun does its best to generate some warmth under the tin roof. It's light and airy inside, and too cool yet for any odor but the scent of pine trees. I take my time, surveying the sturdy lines of the cabin, watching the smoke drift up from the stovepipe that pokes through the neatly shingled roof. It's a good way to be out in the natural light yet out of the weather. It's a great place to bring a book or just to sit, taking time to enjoy the scenery. Best of all, several times a day, it forces me to get out of the cabin. And what's the point of living way out here, if I forget to go outside?

To outhouses then. One of the great inventions of the civilized world.

MENTOR

I can't believe the sound, something lumbering, tearing, crashing through the branches. All the animals here are quiet, so quiet that half the time I don't even notice them. The three deer I see suddenly through the south window have probably been grazing near the creek for hours. Or the coyotes, tawny against the golden wheat stubble, that are always just slipping over the hill as I open the door. Or owls that glide overhead in the dark with bodies so soft and still I barely hear the muffled sigh of air through thick feathers.

So this unexpected clamor is unnatural. The animal must be wounded or rabid or so fierce or large that it can afford to announce its presence in such a bold fashion. I stand immobilized, half terrified, half entranced, and stare at the top of the tallest Ponderosa pine. Branches wave violently. Pine cones drop to the ground. Maybe it's a bear, a brown bear at the very least, if not a misplaced grizzly.

Suddenly, through the thinning lower branches, a shape appears, a big, dark blob against the ruddy-grained trunk. Big and coming down fast, but not big enough to be a bear. A few more feet and it pauses to puff for a moment. I finally realize that the creature—very bushy, a sharp snout—is descending head first.

What can it be? Badgers don't climb trees, do they?

Then I know. It's a porcupine. I can see the quills, a haloed silhouette. I realize that I've never really seen a porcupine before except as a spiny shape in the distance. They are objects of fear, forbidden to dogs and children. I should run, but I don't. How can I pass up this opportunity? Her face is tiny, pointed, delicate. Her feet, too, are tiny and pointed. Her eyes are small and round and very dark. I'd never dreamed there could be anything graceful about such big, lumbering creatures.

With a disdainful glance at me, she continues her way on down the trunk, still head first, still making lots of noise. She reaches the ground, looks at me once more, and waddles off into the woods like those solid-built ladies with very small feet, a size eighteen body teetering on size six high heels.

I call her Quillbutt, even though I soon learn that she deserves a more beautiful, more respectful name. Whenever I hear a loud commotion, I hurry outside so I can watch her charging up or down one of the trees. I am thrilled each time I see her. She seems impossibly constructed, some mythological creature. She's brave and outrageous and unapologetic. She helps me know how wild the wilderness truly is.

Once, at twilight, I come around a corner on the trail and there she is, right in front of me. She must have heard me coming long ago and decided to wait in ambush, prepared, quills puffed out to alarming proportions. She looms large on the trail, bristled and menacing.

I freeze, the instinctive "play dead" behavior of imperiled prey. Then I don't know what to do. All the other animals I've encountered have bolted in terror from the dreadful human, but Quillbutt stands her ground. I can't tell if she is angry or curious or just confident of her defense capabilities. Finally, I bow slightly, respecting her armored solitude, and slowly back away. Still backing up, I veer onto another trail that will take me far to the west of her, and eventually back to the cabin. As I walk, I breathe more freely. Although I've fallen in love with Quillbutt, her delicate clumsiness, her fierceness, her haughty confidence, I've seen the quills embedded in the curious noses of dogs and I have no wish to be struck by her arrows.

Quillbutt is dead. I was gone from the cabin only a few days, and came back to find her spiny skin, the tender flesh already stripped away, along the bank of the creek. They do that here, shoot porcupines. Just for existing. They say the porcupines eat out the tops of the trees, causing the trees to fork instead of growing straight and true for the chain saws. Later, I ask a silviculturist friend about it. He says the damage porcupines do to trees is minimal. Their place in the ecosystem, like the place of most creatures except, perhaps, homo sapiens, is vital. They are valuable citizens of the forest. Any threat they pose is an old logger's tale.

But to the person with the gun, Quillbutt was ugly. Frightening. Arrogant in her armor. Best to shoot her.

I stroke her long quills, no longer dangerous to me. Is this what must happen at the hands of man to all creatures who grow too wild, who lose the ability to conform to civilization? Is it possible to become too different in spiny solitude, too self-assured? Was I wrong to be awed by Quillbutt's strength, wrong to think of her as a kind of mentor, even a friend?

No. I refuse to accept that. Self-sufficiency is essential. Independence is worth any cost. I get to my feet, back straight, head up. I raise what quills I have. I will be strong. I will stand my ground.

SILENCE

We are afraid of silence. We come home from work and turn on the radio even before we get the lights. In the next moment, we play back messages on the answering machine. Start the dishwasher. Switch from the radio to the CD player and nudge up the volume a bit to drown out the heavy metal from the apartment next door. Make dinner to a rock rhythm, then sit down in front of the television. Throughout the evening there is more television, a phone call or two, and the audio companionship of radio announcers, while outside, the din of traffic continues on and an occasional jet roars overhead. Just before bedtime we set the clock radio for an hour of "easy listening" to help us drift off to sleep. We surround ourselves with noise, an ever present guardian against the danger that we might accidentally have an unfiltered, conscious, introspective thought.

I was born an alien into this world of continual noise, some tortured creature from an Edgar Allen Poe story with senses over-keen and vulnerable. I've spent night after wakeful night tormented by a dripping faucet or the relentless bass thumping of someone's stereo or the vibrating roar of an eighteen-wheeler holed up for the night in a vacant lot across the street. Actually, I'm not sure I was born this way. I think my sensitivity to noise has developed gradually over the years. I just happened to fall into occasional moments of pure silence that took on the force of a religious experience.

Silence is still possible in this world, in Idaho especially. Perhaps my initial discovery of silence happened during some adolescent trauma when I went off for a walk all by myself. I moved in velvet dust between two fields in the unusual stillness of the sunset hour. The time of zooming spray planes was over. No one had started harvesting yet. The air was still and the sky was open. The dust muffled the soft thud of my footsteps and the darkness settled around me with scarcely a whisper. I stopped suddenly and felt myself suspended in silence. I realized consciously for the first time what silence sounds like and how powerful it is. The sound of it entered into my ears and stayed there, a benchmark against which all other aural experiences would be measured.

I began to watch for silence and to crave it the way an addict craves her chemical escape. In times of silence, my scattered mind could pull itself back together. The thousand distractions of the day—other people's conversations, the words from songs on the radio, even the rhythms of urban noise—were gone, and I could think with my own thoughts in the rhythm most comfortable to me. I am a slow thinker. I get the punch line two days later. I think in big concepts, vast ideas, that may take days or weeks to sort themselves out. Novels are easy to write because they're big enough. Short stories are difficult and constricting. My mind flows into silence with the same delight that a captive whale, suddenly freed, dives into the vastness of the ocean.

I think I may be ruined now for ordinary life. Maybe I have come home for good to the silence of Idaho and Dead Cow Gulch. Back in the noisy world, it takes a major effort of will to think quick and focused. Like an out of shape athlete, my brain must be poked and prodded to pay attention and keep up. Three days in civilization, four, and I am overcome with longing for Dead Cow Gulch. When at last I am able to go back, I drive with a goofy smile on my face. I park the car at the end of the gravel road and shrug my arms into the straps of my packframe. I start up the narrow tracks through the fields. After only five minutes, past the first switchback, the silence descends around me like the mists of Brigadoon. My body, clenched against the endless barrage of noise, relaxes. My mind sighs and stretches itself and expands to fill the welcoming quiet. Working before in anxious fits and starts like an engine out of synch, my brain slows itself to its natural pace. I smile and walk along and feel the silence enshrouding me and spread my arms to gather the comfort close. I let the silence pull me up the hill and down the other side to home.

LAUGHTER

Humor can be hard for hermits. If I find myself laughing hysterically all by myself in the middle of the wilderness, it often occurs to me that maybe I am just that— hysterical. I'm used to laughter as a social activity.

Laughing is essential, though, for survival out here. Without a sense of humor, I wouldn't have made it past the first month. Usually, I pipe the humor in. I find it in books or in letters from my friends. Every Saturday evening, I listen to Garrison Keillor's "The American Radio Company of the Air." Sometimes I feel like Mr. Keillor is solely responsible for my survival here. His slow, quiet ways mesh perfectly with my slow, quiet life, and then the outrageous bits of humor, the wonderful satire, the illuminating looks at human behavior hit me hard. After two hours of laughing with Garrison Keillor, I feel strong enough to get through another week.

Often I find humor in the perverse workings of my own mind. My brain drifts free out here and sometimes the associations I make offer no recourse save laughter. This laughter does tend a bit toward the hysterical, but I've tried to accept this maniacal side of myself. If I can't entertain myself, how can I expect to entertain anyone else? It's easy, and gratifying, to think of myself as some great mystical ambassador to the wilderness. It takes more practice to celebrate the part of myself that is a buffoon.

Sometimes the creatures here can help to dispel the oh-so-serious aura of art in the process of creation. There is a chipmunk who makes it a habit, every morning, of vaulting onto the screen door, then running around and around its rectangular course, toenails gripping the screen. The raucous sound of it, and the glimpses of frenetic tail, never fail to make me laugh. Later, recuperated from his aerobic workout, he also makes a habit of jumping from the woodshed onto the chamber pot which I lean against the cabin foundation every morning to air out. I believe this is a criticism of my personal hygiene, but it always makes me laugh, too.

After I scream, I always laugh when a frog has jumped out in front of me. Or when a small garter snake goes gliding away into the grass. Mice zipping across the trail. Pheasants catapulting themselves into the air from the brush. Spiders rappelling down onto my head from the outhouse ceiling. Even after months of these startling intrusions, I scream every time, and then I always laugh.

There is the first time or two each winter when I rediscover the properties of frost. Open the door. Step outside onto the ramp. Yikes! Slip. Scream. Plummet. The uselessness of flailing arms. Crash. There are more dignified ways of getting down the ramp.

Or the time I was intent on bringing one more armload of wood into the house before it got completely dark. Locked into the routine, I stack the wood near the stove, step onto the ramp, close the door carefully against the cold and hear the screen door bang shut behind me. But there is an unusual rattling sound. I turn back. The screen door won't open. In a one in a thousand shot, the interior screen door hook has flown up and back down across the nail I use to secure the door from the inside at night. I'm locked out of my own house.

I just need a screwdriver to slide between the door and the frame to pry the hook up. Screwdrivers are inside the house. A thin piece of wire would work. Inside the house. All I have in the way of tools, outside in the growing dark, is the ax. Maybe I'm not that desperate yet. The windows are removable, but securely wedged in place from the inside against the wind. Besides, they're awfully small. Finally, I find a thin but tough twig and manage to get it through the crack. Sure could use a flashlight. Inside the house. After a lot of fumbling, I'm able to nudge the hook up and off the nail. Only then am I able to laugh.

Or the morning, after a great session of writing, I realize I am skipping down the trail. As soon as I notice what I'm doing, I stop. Sheesh! Gone bonkers again. Then I decide I really do feel good enough to skip, but this time I have to consciously dredge up my childhood to remember how to do it. Skipping. Tall, old people forget how good skipping feels.

When I'm writing fiction, I wander around most of the time, muttering. I have conversations with myself about the characters. I act out different scenes. I chop wood the way the protagonist would chop wood, or the villain. I cringe to think what people's reactions would be if they happened to stumble upon me unawares. Actually, it did happen once. Whenever I write, I write with the door closed to create a concentrated space, to prevent any of the ideas from escaping. The closed room is synonymous with my mental state, so focused and intent that nothing else can enter there.

One afternoon, my youngest brother made the mistake of stopping by just as I was into the final rewrite of the final few pages of a very heavy novel. As he opened the door, I turned to face him, wild-eyed, mute, like some unsuspecting creature caught suddenly in the headlights of a car. His own face mirrored the shock and desperation of my crazed features. He mumbled something about checking in later, and disappeared.

We still talk about that sometimes, that I am a mad woman when I write. I am a mad woman, really, when I live. The gift of laughter is the only thing, sometimes, that grounds me, that helps me see how puffed up I've become, how ridiculous. There is nothing like finding myself outside inexplicably preparing to stow my dirty socks in the ice chest to help me get a grip again. I laugh and shake my head and reconnect, at least for a little while, with the real world around me.

MOON SHADOW

I finish the dishes by Braille, trying to feel any last bits of stuck on rice or cheese around the rim of the frying pan. In the shadowed light of candles and propane, it is just too hard to see if the dishes are really clean. Disgusted, I dry the dishes and put them away. Flashlight in hand, I step outside to dump the dishwater. As I turn, something dark stalks me, circling around my legs. I sprint away, but can't shake that black figure hugging the ground. In my fear, I toss the dishpan, and part of the shape breaks off to follow it and then disappears.

It is my shadow. Shadow? In the middle of a winter's night? Then the melody of an old song shapes itself in my throat. "I'm being followed by a moon shadow...moon shadow...moon shadow." I thought that was only a song, strange fancy of cryptic Cat Stevens in a flowery mood. I turn off the flashlight. I look around. The moon is full. It is bright out, brighter than day, bright with a magical, silvery light. It never occurred to me that the moon could get so bright that it could make shadows. But now I see them everywhere, crisp and black against the ground, my shadow, shadow of the cabin, shadow of the smoke rising from the stovepipe. Moon shadow.

I become a devotee of the moon. I mark its phases on my

calendar. I endure the time of the dark of the moon, not minding then if it is cloudy, urging the cloudy nights to come now when there is no moon anyway. After the dark of the new moon, I watch for the first quarter. It begins as a sliver and usually rises in the afternoon while it is still light. It moves quickly across the sky above the hills and quickly sets before it can do any good. But every day, it gets a little bigger and lasts a little longer.

I live for the night of the full moon and the nights on either side of it, trying to conjure up clear skies. Despite the lesson of the stars, I still tend to huddle in the cabin at night, rationing my trips to the outhouse so I only have to stumble outside once or twice through the evening. But now I go out eagerly, carefree, knowing I can see any kind of monster out there long before it can swoop out of the darkness to get me.

In winter, when there is snow for reflection and the moon appears to draw closer to the earth to comfort me, I'm tempted to reverse my schedule. I will sleep during the leaden days when the sky seems to prop itself tiredly against the skylight, and I will live at night, soaking up moon rays. I crave the brightness. I crave the light. On those brightest nights, I could visit the silvered pond. Go for enchanted walks. Even read in the outhouse.

But after only a few days, the moon begins to diminish again. It rises later and later. Soon I've been in bed hours before the moon even appears. Sometimes I forget that it still exists until I turn over in the bunk bed long past midnight and blink at the sudden glare, moon shining in through the skylight. I peer down over the edge of the bunk and see that the moon shadows have come indoors, shapes of the everyday things I use traced on the walls and floor.

Did people really worship the moon? I'm sure they did. How

could they not? It is a great gift of light when light seems to have forsaken the world. I stand outside and lift my hands in gratitude, and the moon paints my homage on the ground behind me. Moon shadow.

FIRE

It's not easy this morning, getting up at Dead Cow Gulch. So far only my nose has ventured out from under the blankets. Then my eyes. The skylight between the rafters a foot or so above my head is frozen over. Not a good sign. But it's light. I can see around the little cabin. The creatures who are my neighbors have probably been awake for hours. It's high time to get up.

Fast is best. Throw off the blankets, wince barefoot down the ladder from the bunk bed, burrow into socks, old sneakers, zippered robe and huge white sweater, my first and only knitting project. Take a moment to use the chamber pot and then turn to the wood stove.

The stove is small because the cabin is small. It squats like a friendly black dog near the door, its cast iron sides molded to show an idyllic scene in the woods. There's nothing that idyllic about 17° above zero. Check both dampers. Open the door with cold-numbed hands. Crinkle up newspaper and spread it over the ashes. Layer the cedar kindling just so, three crisscrossed, two diagonally, and a couple more sticks on top just for luck. Light the match. Watch the flame lick at the paper. Close the door. Wait. Listen. Crouching beside the stove. There should be a sound like wind, the roar of the flames consuming the paper.

Then there should be delicate popping and crackling sounds as the kindling catches. Wait until the sound seems solid. Then open the door. Try to judge the strength of the blaze. Balance two somewhat larger sticks of wood on top of the burning kindling. Close the door again. Wait. Listen. Crouching beside the stove. Slowly feed the fire. Close the damper in the stovepipe slightly.

As the fire takes hold, I relax a little, but I stay at my post. Mistakes are costly. Kill the delicate flame and I have to start all over again, colder now, struggling to clear the half-charred wood out of the way. It is an unforgiving ritual, this kindling of the fire. I shift positions, remembering how bad I was at this the first winter, when I would have given anything for one of those magical thermostat things on the wall that you just turn up and heat starts flowing into the room. I never belonged to the Camp-fire Girls. I never had a fireplace. My only experience with building fires was burning trash in the backyard when I was a kid. I had no idea what a damper was.

The fire sounds sturdy now, robust and happy to consume the fuel I feed it. I open the door and put in the first really big piece of wood, a sixth of a quarter of a huge circle of trunk, the energy of sweat spent hacking it up this summer so I could have the energy of its heat in the winter.

Still tending the fire, listening, checking, slowly closing down the dampers, I start my morning tasks. I climb up onto the desk to make the bunk bed, and then put the ladder on top of the bed out of the way. I get dressed. No fashion statements for the Gulch. Jeans, a T-shirt, a wool shirt over that, two pairs of socks and the ugly red rubber boots I seem to wear most of the time out here, except maybe when I'm in bed.

I stop once more to check the fire. It's settled, the heat of it baking into my bones. The fire will hold now, burning slowly, keeping the cabin warm for hours before I have to deal with it again. I smile an aboriginal smile of pride. I know the fire magic. I've learned the sacred mysteries through the initiation of countless cold mornings. I know by the size and type of wood and the sound and the pattern of flame just what kind of fire it is and how hot it will be and how long it will last, and somehow it is even more magical than that thermostat on the wall.

WIND I

It is the morning of January 8th. About 3:47 a.m. I wake up suddenly, though I realize I've been uneasy for some time. The wind is blowing. No. That's an understatement. The wind is roaring, howling, shoving against the cabin. I've never heard it this loud before. Have I?

I untangle myself from the blankets and turn on the flashlight and climb down the ladder and step into my fur-lined moccasins. It's freezing. I have the usual several pair of socks stuffed into the gaps around the south window, but the wind is pushing through every crack and seam in the cabin as though the walls don't even exist. What is happening? Hands shading my eyes, nose to the glass, I try to see outside, but it is too dark. I get an impression only of black shapes thrashing in the wind. I should go out there, try to figure out what is happening, investigate this storm as I have investigated all the others, but something holds me back. I don't feel up to facing this elemental wind.

And I'm freezing. I pull on my jeans and my thick Idaho sweatshirt with the hood. I find a pair of wool socks. The wind continues to howl. This is such a strange storm. There's no snow; it's not a blizzard, just a dry, relentless wind.

Thinking that there's nothing I can do till morning, fully clothed, I climb back into the bunk bed and try to get warm

again. I'm probably overreacting. I've gotten through all kinds of storms out here before. But even with the sweatshirt hood pulled close around my ears and the blankets over my head, I can still hear the wind. It's so loud. Even more I can feel it. There is a steady pressure against the south and west walls of the cabin. The bunk bed shakes with the sudden gusts. I feel, literally, like I am about to be blown away. I think of the cabin pushed off the small concrete blocks that serve as the foundation and rolling sideways down into the canyon. I think of what will happen to me as the cabin tumbles through the darkness. Will the centrifugal force hold me wedged between the bunk bed and the wall, or will I be tossed around as the cabin rolls, peaked roof, wall, floor, other wall and roof again?

No. That's ridiculous. Houses, even small ones, don't blow away. Still, I catch myself adding up the interior weight of the cabin—the cast iron wood stove, the computer, my unabridged dictionary. Every ten minutes or so for the next two hours I climb back out of the bunk bed and stand vigil on the floor below. With the flashlight off, I can see the trees a little more clearly. They twist and bend and gyrate in the wind, fighting for their lives. I watch them, thinking that I should be on my feet too, ready to face whatever is to come.

But each time, after only a few minutes, I'm so cold I climb back into the sanctuary of the bed. I listen through the growing crescendo of the next onslaught. Surely this will be the last gust. Surely the wind will die down after this. But each gust seems harder. The cabin shudders. The bunk bed vibrates with the force pushing against it. I cling to the wooden frame, like a castaway clinging to her bit of wreckage, riding out each wave of wind.

Finally, exhausted by the noise and my own fear, I sink into a kind of frozen oblivion. I'm still aware of tensing for imminent destruction with every gust, and then relaxing a little each time the worst passes and I seem to be intact. A couple of times I seem to hear the sharp crack of explosions. I can't imagine what could make a sound like that. Maybe this is the end of the world. I am ashamed, thinking that I will spend the last few minutes before eternity cowering in my bed. I thought I was braver than this.

Around 6:00, the wind begins to slow a little. My clenched limbs relax. I actually fall asleep, stunned that I have survived the night and made it through till morning. My brother wakes me up, pounding on the locked door. He has driven all the way out here to see if I'm all right.

I am startled and half asleep and disoriented. The wind is still blowing, down now to about 35 m.p.h. from a high of 84 m.p.h. gusts. I am lost in my brother's words—trees down everywhere, power out, buildings demolished, phones dead. Past him, through the windows, I can't recognize the landscape. Everything seems jumbled, off kilter. I think maybe some of my trees have gone down, and quickly look away. No. That can't be.

My brother leaves to cut his way through other roads and check on the rest of the family. I dress more completely and step out onto the ramp. The wind pushes against me so hard it's difficult to open my eyes enough to see. But I do see. The stovepipe is lying on the ground. The outhouse has been toppled over onto its back and lies prostrate in the dead grass, the cut out circle of the seat like a big dark mouth crying for help.

And there are trees down. I see the gaps, and can't bear to look, and yet can't escape the knowledge. Not just trees, but favorite trees. The pine that arched so gracefully across the creek, the one I watch from my desk through the east window, snapped off half way up. Another tree, a tree I never really noticed before because it was just one of the many huge, straight,

Ponderosa pines, nothing distinguishing about it—but what a huge hole it has left, broken off ten feet or so above the ground, its massive body shattered along the hillside on the other side of the creek, dwarfing the other, smaller trees that were pulled down with it.

And then the third tree, the one I cannot bear to admit is gone. It is the elephant tree, my favorite tree, the one tree I picked especially to be my own. I first noticed it because of the way the morning sun touched its reddish Ponderosa skin and made it shine, ruddy and rich. Then I discovered the big lump on the southern side, a huge tumor, a barked over wound from some dreadful experience the tree must have suffered when it was just starting to grow. Below this big "head," two bleached branches hung down like tusks. But above the abnormality, the tree stretched up, straight and tall and proud as all the others, overcoming its childhood trauma. The tree was huge and old and odd, so wonderful to watch through the changing light of every day and season.

And now it is gone. The fierce night's wind has torn it asunder right at the wounded place, leaving only a jagged stump. I finally see the rest of it, the straight growth and the wondrously gnarled tumor, fallen in splintered bits in the creek.

I go inside. I sit down at the desk, trying not to look out the windows and see what I have just seen. The trees. The beautiful trees. My stomach clenches with denial. This is still part of the nightmare. The trees can't really be gone. Then I put my head down on the desk and cry.

TOOLS

The first tool I made out here was a water carrying stick. The stick I found was long and thin and slightly curved. I peeled off the bark and whittled the knobs from other smaller branches smooth with my jackknife. Then I set out for the spring with two water jugs, carrying the filled jugs back suspended across my shoulders like a peasant woman carrying buckets on a yoke. I felt a little embarrassed, like maybe this primitive living stuff had gone too far, and yet I also felt smug. With the water carrying stick I could haul twice as much water much more comfortably. When I got inside, I leaned the stick in the corner and it's been there ever since. A tool.

An old piece of barn board pointed on one end. It was quickly obvious to me that this particular piece of wood, carried in with other scrap lumber for the stove, was actually a poker. I use it to nudge and prod the wood into burning better. I use it to lever the bigger logs back in the stove so I can get the door shut. Actually, this is my second poker. One of my friends, not recognizing the first poker as a tool, added it to the fire one winter afternoon.

I suppose I have tools everywhere that don't really look like tools. The outhouse rock. The knot-infested circle of pine that is my chopping block. The piece of kindling I keep in the outhouse to squash ticks with. The little hunk of bark that works perfectly to wedge the door open in summer. I feel tribal, related to my ancestors, when I adapt the organic things around me to make my life better.

I tend to think of tools in the broadest sense, as human ingenuity operating in a problematic world. Tools are mental solutions made visible. In a 9 by 12 foot cabin, space is at a premium. I needed a place for paper towels. So I carved the shape of a nail into the side of a piece of kindling. Then I toenailed the nail into the wall. I settled the stick on top of the nail and lashed it into place. I settled the cardboard roll over the stick. Voilá! A paper towel dispenser. This was my first made, as opposed to found, tool. I could do something much more elaborate now, but I keep the original dispenser because I was so proud of myself when I first constructed it. I like to look at it and see how far I've come.

The skylight really does leak. Often. My usual solution was to put a bucket under it. Unfortunately, the leak is right over the desk. On bad days, I had to twist my chair sideways and try to work with the water plunking relentlessly into the bucket beside me, often splashing out onto the paper. Chinese water torture. It made me crazy.

One grey day, after hours of dripping with no letup in sight, I stretched out on the floor. It was shaping up to be one of those—Why am I doing this?—What have I gotten myself into?—afternoons. Absently, I stared at the unfinished ceiling. I studied the skylight, watching each drop fall past the rafters and make the long plunge into the bucket. I noticed the cobwebs draped along the ceiling shelf near the wood stove. Then I looked again.

How was the shelf constructed? Six wide flat boards laying across the rafters. The board closest to the stovepipe wasn't really usable because it got so hot there. Weren't there rafters on either side of the skylight? Wouldn't that extra board fit just as well across those rafters as where it was now? If I put a long, rectangular pan on top of that board, wouldn't the pan catch the drips from the skylight? If the water only had to fall a few inches, wouldn't it land quieter than it did now? If the receptacle was way overhead, wouldn't I have my whole desk again for work instead of having to share it with a bucket?

It seemed rational. I tried it. It worked. I spent the rest of the afternoon, productively, at my desk, a triumphant grin on my face. The leak was still there, but at least the symptoms were manageable, the way you take Contac and know you still have a cold, but at least you're not as miserable anymore. Tools are like that.

I like real tools, too. I inherited my grandfather's awl, and ever since that time, I have taken pride in putting up towel racks and pencil sharpeners all across America. First you mark the place where the bracket should go. Then you drill a hole smaller and shorter than the screw. Then you insert the screw and tap it gently with a hammer to set it so it will go in straight. Then you slowly screw it in, being careful not to strip the head.

This is a man thing, "the proper way to screw," something I picked up from my dad and brothers. Tools are man things, clever objects invented to make jobs easier. Or possible. I used to move from apartment to apartment, trying to set up housekeeping without tools. I would pound nails into walls with the heel of a shoe. I would try to pry things open with a kitchen knife.

Now I have a whole collection of tools. A good hammer. Screw drivers in several sizes, both slotted and Phillips. The awl. A crescent wrench. A tape measure. Pliers. A pipe wrench. A putty knife. An ax. A hatchet.

Tools are power. Once Dad was helping me with something and asked for a screwdriver. When I gave it to him, he hefted it in his hand. "Pretty diminutive, isn't it?" I went out and bought

65

another, non-diminutive screwdriver that same day. Tools can be woman things, too. They should be sturdy and strong enough to get the job done. One of my friends admitted to having a hammer with pink sparkles in the handle. They may try to make women's tools look frivolous, but as long as the hammer is good-sized and well-balanced, the pink sparkles won't keep us from getting the job done. We deserve quality tools. Using cheap tools just ensures that we stay helpless.

I like tools. They add to my confidence. So much of my work is cerebral, it makes me happy when I can do some piece of work that is real and physical. I like the creativity of finding solutions for the stupid little problems that make the difference between a pleasant, productive life and a cranky, inefficient one. Right now, the skylight isn't leaking and I'm certainly not complaining. But even if it does start again, at least I know I have a solution that will let me keep working at my desk until I can figure out a more permanent way to fix the problem.

UNIVERSITIES

niversity of Idaho? Actually, there are two of them. There is the physical, geographical University of Idaho, and there is the UI that is a mental state. For the past year, I have lived in both places. On weekdays I teach writing classes for the English Department, caught up in the frenzy of manufactured learning—lesson plans, meetings, conferences with students, discussions with colleagues, hurried assaults on the library. On weekends, and through the summer, I retire to Dead Cow Gulch to attend that other university, the UI of the mind.

"Why do you do it?" my friends ask me. "How can you stand it?" They visualize the difficulties. No electricity. No running water. Cold, dark trips to the outhouse late at night. The half hour hike in and then back out to the car. Making meals without an oven or a refrigerator or a microwave. Hauling all that water for a less than successful washtub bath and shampoo. The lack of civilized amenities, even the sanctioned professorial escape of PBS.

It's hard to answer their objections in words. I'd probably go back to that milestone semester when I took the Thoreau class and only five additional credits. After seven semesters of at least an eighteen-credit load and a part-time job, in that last UI semester, I finally discovered what it means to learn. Classes are the launching point, a brief period filled with the intellectual white heat of knowledge acquisition, but learning is forever. Consuming knowledge and digesting that knowledge are two different things.

The morning sun pierces the prism hanging at the east window and paints colors on the cabin walls. From the bunk bed I watch the small room take shape—the desk and straight-back chair below me, the counter along the west wall that serves as a kitchen, the filing cabinet, the wood stove. The whole day is mine. No schedule. No phone. No interruptions. I don't shape the time here so much as it shapes me. Half an hour lost in reverie gazing at the pond. The trout are secretive today. While I watch for them, a school of ideas gathered through the last few days sort themselves, find connections, and break the surface of my mind. The week, lived on fast forward, can be played back slowly out here, and what was gibberish begins to have meaning. There is time for savoring, reflection, and revelation.

The sun continues to shine. The solar panel sucks in that silent power and feeds it to the small computer on the desk. Strange intrusion of technology? Not really. After all these years of living intimately with me, the computer has become organic. It waits patiently for me to find the words. It holds them, scroll-like, and lets me roll the paragraphs back and forth, moving sentences around like images in a painting until everything fits. Writing is the child born of the union of knowledge and thought, the place where my two universities come together.

Evening. I lay the hatchet aside, taking a break from the steady "sproing, sproing" rhythm of kindling shooting free from the dry, straight-grained cedar, and sit down on the chopping block. The silence here is so pronounced it is like a sound. I hear the fact that I hear nothing. Freed from the din of civilized life, my ears pick up the faintest whisper of wind through the pines

overhead, the secretive rustlings of a field mouse behind me, an undercurrent of life's murmuring that medievalists referred to as the music of the spheres. I go by the "s" words out here—slow, space, silence, solitude. Though I probably need the stimulation of the physical university, only on Dead Cow Gulch do I have the time and horizons and quiet and isolation to tap into the true power of my mind. If the other university offered only one more class, I would propose Silent Meditation 101.

"Simplify! Simplify!" Thoreau exhorted all those years ago, and I obey him. Again, I'm not sure I can explain why I live this way and how much it means to me. I think most people would have to try it and spend a year, as I did, getting over their material addictions before they could begin to understand. Meanwhile, I'll probably continue my doubled life, taking the best from both universities, the one in Moscow and the one I've discovered out here.

WIND II

It has been two months since the night of the big wind. I walk through the slushy snow toward the cabin, and just like all the times before, my stomach hurts and my throat aches on seeing the changed landscape. My skyline is irrevocably altered, a place of gaps and the sundered torsos of trees where lovely pines should be growing. Will it ever stop hurting? Will I ever reconcile myself to the loss of the trees?

I came here to live with nature. I realize now that I wanted nice nature, Disney nature—spring flowers, cuddly animals, technicolor sunsets. I wanted a nature that was free of the violence and the random cruelty of man that had darkened my spirit in the civilized world.

I live on in the cabin, but I feel betrayed. Nature, too, is cruel. She wreaks havoc on her own creatures and leaves their bodies to rot. What other things that I have grown to love will she take from me? She is mindless, subject to fits of destruction—cold, wind, rain, fire, drought. If life here is savage and life out there is savage, what is the point of living at all? There is no safe place on the planet, no place that is free of evil and hurt.

I suppose it is worse because I fought so hard to save the trees. Last summer, the owners decided to log the canyon. They didn't want to clear-cut it, for which I was extremely grateful, but just to thin the trees to earn money and, as the foresters put it, to ensure the health of the woods. So I spent the whole summer cringing at the sound of chain saws, praying that the loggers would remember they weren't supposed to cut down all the trees, leaving pathetic little notes taped to their bulldozers that begged them not to take any more of the trees around the cabin.

To save the trees from humans, whose habits of destruction I had come, bitterly, to accept, only to lose them to nature, seemed too cruel to bear. It also nagged at me that the trees had been lost because I had failed to protect them, because I had stayed inside that night afraid for my own life instead of going outside to stand vigil with them in their struggle to survive the unexpected wind. Every time I look at them now, I see their pain in the twisted wood fibers of the jagged stumps, proof of how hard the upper reaches of the trees fought to cling to life. I feel guilt and loss and sorrow without end.

WOUNDS

My brother and I are loading the small shed he helped me build onto the truck to haul it down to the cabin. We don't have it quite balanced and it slides back off, the edge of the tin roof slicing through my arm at the elbow as the shed falls. The pain feels like heat. Alarms go off in my brain. "The body has been hurt! The body has been hurt!" I feel numb, a little shaky.

I look down and there is a long curved angry line snaking around the bend of my right arm. Even as I watch, the line turns bright red and then overflows.

"Are you all right?"

"Yeah, sure. Just a scratch."

We've been working in the shop, that male domain, all morning. I know I'm supposed to be macho about this, shrugging off the injury even as I'm thinking about stitches and a trip to the Emergency Room. We lift the heavy lean-to like structure again and get it onto the truck while blood drips down on my jeans. Only after we've loaded all the tools does my brother take a few minutes to wash away the blood and tape one of those big gauze pads over the cut.

Wounds. When I lived in the city, I never got hurt. A paper cut every once in a while. An occasional hangnail. But out here at the cabin, I have little injuries all the time. Slivers. Blisters. Bruises. Mashed fingers. Cuts. Sore muscles. Burns. Scrapes. Bug bites. My body is no longer invulnerable. Instead, it is a living part of the environment and subject to all the violences of life and nature.

When I lived in the city, I stood or I sat or I lay down. My body was almost always locked into one of those three postures. Here in the woods I find my body flowing through all kinds of positions. I crouch, squat, reach, bend, kneel, climb, lift, carry, crawl. The old delicate movement of adjusting the thermostat is replaced by those rhythmic, powerful swings at the chopping block and the crouched intensity of starting the fire. The act of turning on the faucet is now an uphill walk to the spring and the slow return with the pull on my shoulders of brimming water jugs.

My body feels alive the way it never felt alive in the city. Instead of the made up work of aerobics, my body goes through all the motions of the real work I need to do to survive. It was easy to skip aerobics, but if I don't split wood this afternoon and carry it inside to dry a bit more by the stove, tomorrow will be a pretty cold and miserable day. If I don't haul water today, it's bound to rain tonight, and then I'll have to push through all that wet, waist-high grass to get water in the morning.

After a whole winter of sitting hunched in the outhouse shivering, it's indescribably pleasant to stroll out there in my shirt sleeves and prop the door open and bask in the sun. After an unusual heat spell, several sweaty nights of sleeping nude and uncovered up in the bunk bed, it's lovely when the regular Idaho weather returns, the cool currents of night air settling around me so I can snuggle again under my blankets.

"But aren't you scared being way out there all alone?" people ask me. "What if you get hurt? What if you get sick?"

That seems to be the hardest thing for others to understand. It doesn't even help when I suggest that I could be doing something really dangerous like living in New York or working sixty hours a week at a high-stress job.

Actually, I do get scared. The time I fell off the ladder while I was shingling the woodshed and landed on the propane tank, I was scared. I lay on the ground for a long time. I couldn't breathe so good. I thought I might have broken my back. But after a while, I got to my feet. Everything seemed to work. I did have kind of a dent in my backside that eventually turned into a technicolor bruise, but no other ill effects. I considered myself lucky. It had been a gentle warning. Now I'm very careful about setting up the ladder. No heroics. I take responsibility for my own safety.

There's a kind of power that comes from being in charge of my own life. I've learned the lessons of survival. I've figured out solutions. I've gotten myself through the periods of loneliness and cabin fever. The few times I've been sick, I've nursed myself back to health.

It's risky, yes. The next tree that falls in a big windstorm could fall on the house instead of away from it. The next stick I pick up could be the rattlesnake that does me in. If the skylight starts leaking again, my latest attempt to climb up on the roof and patch it could end in disaster. But living here is worth the risk. It's worth it because I *am* living, aware almost all the time of my self and my body and the woods around me. I'm proud of the curving scar on my arm and the other marks of my life out here. They are badges of honor. They are proof that I've chosen to live rather than just exist. Life is risky for anyone who is alive, and anyone who wants to truly live, must be willing to take those risks. These small dangers faced give an edge to life that makes it all the more precious. The trade-off, so far, has been well worthwhile.

GHOST FLOWERS

I walk on. Stop. Go back. Were they there, or weren't they? I search the ground. Finally I see them. Look away. Look back. They're gone. It's June and the ghost flowers have returned once more.

I shrug out of the pack frame and lay it aside. I crouch down and try to figure out the magic again, just like last year and the year before. Ghost flowers. Tiny white things growing in clumps close to the ground. They're not daisy-petaled—she loves me, she loves me not—though they give that impression from a distance. Close up, the flowers are minuscule and they're in little three petal clusters. These tiny clusters are arranged around the stem in ways that could seem like petals.

I stand up. The illusion of petals returns, but now I can see the tiny spaces between the clusters, the absence of white. Perhaps it is these gaps in what my eyes perceive as uniform petals that make the flowers fade in and out of my vision.

I crouch down again. The flowers instantly assume their true shape. But this time I see something else. The minute tri-petals are not pure white. Rather, they are white veined with faintest lavender. They are shaded with tints of lavender so delicate as to be almost invisible.

I stand once more. I strain to glimpse the purple. But all I see

76

is the shifting of the flowers from there to not there and back again. They are still ghost flowers, even if I am beginning to know their secrets. Shouldering my pack, I continue on down the trail to the cabin.

It is astonishing, the time I have here for minutiae. Sometimes, smallness is all I can truly see. The big things of nature—the sunsets, the thunderstorms, the acres of trees—can be too big. I can't grasp them. I can't take them in. What is small seems more accessible, but even the wonder of the tiny things can be overwhelming. Like the hunt for the crickets.

It is impossible that anyone could make music by rubbing their legs together, especially such loud, piercing songs as those of the cricket. I can hear them outside, just beyond the ramp, singing joyfully in the morning sun. I'm suddenly possessed with the necessity of finding out how they do that. So I sneak out onto the ramp. As always, the songs go silent the moment I approach, the evil human, the other, the walker on large dangerous feet.

I sit down cross-legged in the grass. I make myself still. I wait. One by one, the songs start up again. But how will I locate and recognize the singers? People call those hideous black things I've seen crickets, the kind that hop alarmingly about in damp basements, the kind that homeowners flatten on cement floors. But those must be common crickets. Singing crickets would wear little waistcoats, wouldn't they, or at least they'd be a lovely warm brown or beautifully golden colored.

I wait, surrounded by song. And then, less than a foot away, I see a cricket, the big black basement variety. I hold my breath. I lean a little closer. The song is coming from him. It is. I stare and I stare and the legs are moving. They vibrate, rubbing together faster than I can see, but the rhythm of that vibration matches the rhythm of the song. I stay a long time, entranced, believing what I see and yet not able to believe it. Nature is beyond human. She knows no bounds.

Then there was the afternoon of the slugs. I pass them, two dusty tan slugs in a dusty tan patch of dirt in the trail. They are paler than most Idaho slugs I've seen and slightly larger. And there are two of them. And they are moving in a circle. Aren't they? I stop and watch. They are, head to tail and head to tail, following each other in a circle. They've generated a little lake of slug slime and they glide around the perimeter of it. They move slowly, as all slugs must move, and yet with a definite purpose.

Eventually, little single horns protrude from the sides of their bodies just behind the head. They wave the horns and try to prod each other with them, sometimes head to tail, sometimes head to head. I sit down. What is going on? The circular dance continues. The prodding continues. Is this some kind of slug fight, male against male? Or is it slug sex? Are they locked into some kind of sensual dance in an effort to procreate?

I watch and I watch, waiting for something to happen. I leave for a few minutes and come back. Are they a little more frenetic? Are we approaching some kind of climax? I wait. I watch. It's starting to get dark. I think about bringing a candle out to continue my vigil. That would be romantic for them, wouldn't it, not an intrusion? The pattern of circling and probing continues. If there is a change, it is too small for me to sense it. My left leg goes to sleep. I think about what I was going to have for supper. Finally, some old habit of clocks and productivity pushes me to my feet. I can't spend the night with them, after all. I watch for a few more seconds and then go inside.

The next morning I find the place, a shiny, stained circle in the dust. Both slugs are gone. There is no hint of what finally happened. I've never again stumbled upon two circling slugs, but I'll never stop watching for them. Nature is full of mysteries, large and small, and I'll be a lifetime unraveling just a few of them.

TICKS

I hum to myself as I ease down the steep hill into the canyon. It's a warmish day in spring and I'm wearing sneakers instead of my boots. First time this year. I know it's too soon. I'll end up tiptoeing around bogs and mud wallows most of the way. But I don't care. Freed from those ugly boots and my heavy coat, I feel like a new person. I glance down to enjoy the liberty of my feet and count eight, nine, no, eleven ticks scurrying up my pantlegs.

Hmm. I forgot about you guys. I flick off a particularly enthusiastic one. It's not a Lyme disease tick or a Rocky Mountain spotted fever tick, just one of the fifteen to twenty plain old Idaho ticks, attached or still looking, that I will find on myself most every day now until the weather gets hot enough in late May or June. I brush all eleven ticks off, though I know this is pointless, and continue on my walk.

Back home, I make a pit stop at the outhouse. I find a couple of ticks and dispatch them quickly and ruthlessly. Ticks are hard to kill. Their tough, rubbery bodies can take a lot of punishment. Step on one and they just shake themselves, climb up and around the heel of your shoe and bite you in the ankle. On the way to the cabin, I take off my flannel shirt and shake it vigorously. Inside, I strip off my outer clothes and parade in front of the mirror.

There's one on my thigh. One at the bend of my knee. One on my back that I can just barely reach. I flick them on the counter one by one, squish them with a pair of tweezers and put them in the wood stove. With those out of the way, I comb my hair thoroughly and go back to the mirror to spot a few more. Then I examine my jeans, front and back and inside out. I do the same thing with my T-shirt. Satisfied that I've de-infested myself, I put my clothes back on and sit down at the desk to get to work.

Tick killing wasn't always so easy for me. At first, I tried to be nice to them. But every tick I let go would inevitably find its way back to me. They are full of blood lust in the spring. I am the biggest breakfast around and they are fiercely hungry.

I twitch in my chair. There's a strange sensation on my left shoulder. I get up, pull off my shirt, and sure enough, there's another of the little devils. These tick-lish interruptions will go on for the next couple of hours. It's a skill I've developed, an acute sensitivity to weightless, eight-legged contact with my skin. I pride myself on the fact that ticks hardly ever have time to get attached. I always sense them before they can burrow in for the feast.

I'm making good progress this morning. Chapter seven is almost ready to print. Absently, I run my fingers through my hair. There's a bump up there. An eight-legged bump. A bump that moves. Damn. I grab my comb and pull it hard against my scalp, bending over the counter so I can see when the tick drops out. But nothing falls. Gingerly, I reach up to feel that place on my head. The tick is still there. Attached. The last time I had a stuck-on tick in my hair, I happened to be at the home farm and Mom got it out for me.

So what do I do? I just got here. I wasn't planning to go back out to civilization for three more days. But how do I deal with this tick? It really grosses me out to think of it up there happily sucking the blood from my brain. My methods have improved with experience. When I was a kid, we used the hot knife method. You heat a knife on the burner and then hold it near the tick. In an attempt to escape the heat, the tick usually lets go and backs out so you can nab it. Then you put it on the hot burner and watch it blow up. (I've largely dispensed with this sadistic part of the ritual.) Unfortunately, it's hard to use this method when you're alone, especially for ticks in difficult locations. The first time I had an armpit tick, I knew I had to find another way.

Lately, I've been doing this. I place the tweezers just so and squeeze the tick's body, but not so hard that I kill it. Usually, the pain makes the tick let go and then I slowly draw it out of my skin. Sometimes, even then, it holds on tenaciously and I end up removing a little plug of my own flesh as well. The important thing is to get the head. If you leave the head of a dismembered tick in your skin, like the one I left in the back of my leg, it gets badly infected and takes weeks to heal. I always watch carefully to make sure I'm getting the whole thing.

Back to my present problem. I make a few attempts at grabbing the tick embedded in my scalp, but I can't see it and all that hair is in my way. I can't think what to do. I try combing again, but that tough little guy is not going to be deterred by a few plastic teeth scraping across his back. I guess I'll just have to leave it in there for these three days until I can get some help. It doesn't seem like there's any other option.

I try to go back to work, but all I can think about is that tick up there. I know that in a day, two days, it will swell way up with my blood, a huge, bloated thing, its dark brown body stretched to pale tan. I can't bear it. I pace around the cabin, trying to decide what to do. It seems ridiculous to walk for half an hour and drive seventeen miles because of a stupid bug, and yet.

Then I remember this story I read once. This guy was doing

some kind of Alaskan wilderness adventure. He went out for his morning dump, wiped himself and found a tick in the worst imaginable place. He was truly alone. He had to find some kind of solution. Finally, he took a big glob of lard and slathered it over the affected area. After about fifteen minutes, the tick ran out of air and disengaged.

Hmm. I don't have any lard. I don't even have shortening. Would vaseline work? I get a big glob on my finger. My hair is fairly clean. I hate to smear grease into it, but I have to do something. With the trembling fingers of my left hand, I locate the tick. Then I spread the vaseline on top of him. I wait, pacing again. Finally, I feel some movement up there. I grab a wad of toilet paper, center it in place, clamp my fingers together hard and pull.

I got it! The tick lays in the toilet paper, shiny and gasping for breath. I show it no mercy. Into the fire it goes. I strut around for a little while, still shaking but proud that I could take charge of such a horrifying situation. It occurs to me that courage is really only the result of awful choices. We can all do impossibly brave things if the alternative is even worse. Relieved, I make one last check in front of the mirror and go back to work.

TOPOGRAPHY

People from Kansas would go crazy here. The vistas of the sky are huge, but the land itself is rounded. It flows, curves, undulates and folds over onto itself. It is a land of draws and benches and hollows and saddles and canyons and bluffs. No matter how high I climb, there are always places I cannot see, hidden clefts and the nether sides of hills that are hidden from me. I don't have that clear, unobstructed view of prairies or deserts or ocean beaches.

But I should go back a ways. About 15 million years. First lava flows laid the basalt foundation. Then for centuries, acres and acres of volcanic loess soil blew over the area and settled in great, black mounds. Fortunately, when 400 cubic miles of water roared out of a massive lake in Montana 18,000 to 20,000 years ago, the wall of water by-passed this region and left the huge hills intact. When pioneers first started farming here, the topsoil was 20 feet deep in places. This unique geological sequence happened only in a small unique area, the 4000 square miles of northern Idaho and eastern Washington known as the Palouse.

The boundaries of the Palouse are easily discernible. The soil changes from an incomparably fertile, dark brown to tan, and trees grow far more abundantly than the man-high grasses that once covered the region. From the rich Palouse soil, farmers coax

incredible yields, but on the edges, they are giving up and letting the land go back to trees whose tougher roots can poke down through the hardpan 6-12 inches below the surface and thrive.

So that is where I live, amidst the rounded rubbish heaps of ancient volcanoes. I am often lost. Go down any hill and I am instantly swallowed up by the land. It curves up and around me, hill upon hill, soft rounded shapes that all look the same. There is only one real landmark, big, blue Moscow Mountain to the north. If I can climb high enough to see that, I have a chance of finding my way home again.

Even though this land is spacious and huge, sometimes I long for a cleaner view, the stark clarity of the desert or the down-to-earth flatness of Midwest fields. Perhaps I would see better there, not get so muddled up in all that is hidden and all the things that lie just beyond my sight. This land is illusive, mysterious, full of dark secrets. It is rarely straightforward in what it tells me. I must climb and descend and circle back and catch sight of something only to lose it and then begin the search all over again. The truths I find here are hard won.

And yet I love this curvaceous land. It is voluptuous. It is seductive. In early spring I go outside and climb the hill to the north and stretch out on top of it, knees bent, my vinyl coat protecting me from the damp earth. The feeble spring sun warms me. The spring wind, still cold, blows higher up, dipping only occasionally to brush past my face. I relax in the warmth and feel the roundness of the land spreading beneath me. I roll over onto my stomach and stretch out my arms. I embrace the land, this round hill, kin with the myriad rolling hills of the Palouse, which in turn lie adjacent to other lands that all curve round and round this great globe I ride on. It is a gentle, nurturing topography with strong basalt bones underneath and I ride lightly on its surface and it supports me well.

NATURE

Nature sure is natural. That's the first thing I learned. And in spite of all the idealistic reasons I've given for doing this, today I must admit that I have no business being here. In Idaho. Living in this cabin out on Dead Cow Gulch. Although I really was born and raised in Genesee, Idaho, I've spent a lot of time in cities—Seattle, Bellingham, Hartford, Syracuse. Nature is very civilized in cities. Since almost everything is paved over, dust exists only under beds. There are no gravel roads, let alone dirt ones. Parks are carefully manicured and don't, as a general rule, have rattlesnakes. Pollution levels keep the bugs to a minimum. Swat a couple of flies in early spring and that's about it.

But even before the years of city living, I knew I was not genetically designed for Idaho. There are farmers on both sides of the family for generations back, but as far as I've been able to determine, I haven't inherited a single farmer gene. During those endless summer mornings in the garden as I pulled weeds and picked peas with dainty and anxious fastidiousness lest I get a single molecule of dirt on my fingers, I knew with complete certainty that I was adopted. I was the daughter of concert pianists who had given me up for the sake of their careers. I was the illegitimate offspring of a tempestuous affair between the leading players of a touring Shakespearean company stranded, temporarily and improbably, in Idaho. Not only adopted, but British as well. No wonder I didn't fit in with these peasants. (The fact that I looked exactly like my grandmother and my father made it a bit difficult to sell this theory of adoption, but I persisted.)

As I lifted each raspberry leaf to peer underneath before risking my hands in that jungle darkness teeming with unseen spiders and other assorted vermin, I knew that I was destined for finer things. All through my childhood, I wondered what cruel trick of fate sent me trudging out to the endless garden rows instead of skipping down some block to the grocery store, that magical place filled with produce so perfect it didn't even look real, vegetables that must have been created in some kind of immaculate conception having absolutely nothing to do with dirt.

So why am I really here in this tiny cabin surrounded by bugs and dust, mud and darkness? As I said, the reasons vary, depending on my mood. Today, bereft of my usual environmental glow, I can think of three. Laziness. Perversity. Roots. Out in the urban world, people didn't seem to recognize my innate gentility either. They thought I should slave away for money just like everyone else. But that was dreadful. I had to put in hours and hours at really demanding jobs to earn enough money to live in the fashion to which I knew I should have been accustomed. At least when I live cheap like this, I don't have to work so hard.

I am naturally perverse. When I lived on the farm, I thought Idaho was the whole world, and that cities were a fiction created for books. Now I know that cities are everywhere and spreading fast, and that Idaho is the true rarity. There is a sort of elitist pleasure in stealing these few years of solitude from Idaho's crowded future.

And roots. Maybe I'm not adopted after all. I seem to at least have inherited the farmer's love for the land and open spaces. I liked the city but could never really live there. I'd been too contaminated, early on, by that blue, open, Idaho sky. So I came back.

It hasn't been easy though. I am daily horrified by each new act of nature. She marches right along without the slightest regard for my trembling sensibilities. To the spider in bed with me this morning, I was just another common lump in its geography. A condensed audio recording of my first months here would sound like the gasping, shrieking, screaming audience at a horror flick. A big June bug in the outhouse. Really big. Frogs and mice and garter snakes startling me every time I walk up to the spring to get water. A fat-bodied spider living near the ice chest. Those dirty-grey moths my family has always called "millers" fluttering a kamikaze dive into my breakfast enchiladas. Worms. Slugs. Maggots. Ticks. Yellow jackets. Stink bugs. Dust storms that seem determined to deposit the topsoil of the entire west field on my desk. Day after day after day of mud. The frozen outhouse seat on winter mornings.

But living on Dead Cow Gulch is probably good for me. Nature chips away at my arrogance. Out here I'm forced to dismiss my delusions of grandeur and accept that I'm just one small piece of life at the mercy of forces stronger than I'll ever be. Though deep inside I'll probably always cling to the belief that someday my "real" parents will claim me, that someday I'll get to be as rich and famous as I've always assumed I should be, living here forces me to be a bit more honest. Well, at least some of the time.

There's a sudden loud noise just overhead. Oh no. One of those big buzzy bugs, a large rough-coated beetle that looks like a piece of bark. If they just crawled around, I suppose I could ignore them, but they fly. Big-bodied things, they buzz around alarmingly and then plop down hard. I hate the thought of having to deal with this creature, but if I don't, I'll spend the rest of the afternoon keeping a wary eye on it and dodging its clumsy puddle jumps from bunk to desk to wall. With a sigh, I get up to gather my bug removal tools. Nature sure is natural.

MIDDLE GROUND II

More than two years on the Gulch and I am still living in the middle ground, a place suspended between civilization and wilderness. I walk through the chemical fields to get here, following a road made by trucks and tractors. I leave the same way, following the dirt road until it becomes gravel. There I get into the car and drive off to town.

My alfalfa field still looks like an alfalfa field. In the ten years since it was left to grow wild, I count only eight pine saplings sprouting up, the tallest about seven feet, the smallest about five inches. Ten years to engender eight small trees. Nature works slowly to reclaim her territory. There is a single blackcap bush on the grass-grown hillside. How much longer to create the thorny tangle that becomes home to so many small animals?

And what about me? Do I take the road to civilization too often, rather than the shadowed road into the canyon? Do I cling too closely to my civilized ways? A clean, dry place to work and eat and sleep. The morning news on NPR. Store bought food. Deodorant. Toothpaste. Will the wilderness ever be able to reclaim my heart, engender a pine tree there or the tangled canes of blackcaps? How many years will I have to stay here before the wilderness makes its claim on me?

I am tempted. Some days the struggles with water and heat

and light and food wear me down. Some days the packframe is almost too heavy to lift, filled with all the things I think I will need here and refilled with all the things I have to haul out. Am I to be a pack mule all my life? How much easier to give in to the lure of wildness. I'll get rid of my contact lenses and see with my own eyes. I'll learn to frolic on the warm days and hunker down on the cold ones, waiting out the storms. In winter, instead of fretting about the loss of light and productivity, I'll just sleep more, that wonderful cozy sleep of conscious laziness. I'll get back all the senses that I've lost—where the good water is and how much time I have before the weather changes and what's out there to eat today. I'll live in nature instead of only with nature.

And yet I am afraid to cross over that line. I see the simple freedom of the animals and I long for that lost part of my life, but my mind cries out—books, friends, movies, the pleasure of dining, the bone-baking heat of fire warmth, the lovely feel of a hot shower and clean clothes.

So I'm stuck on the middle ground. I'm not wild enough to give up my civilized pleasures. My civilized pleasures keep me from becoming truly wild. My heart needs Mozart and yet listening to Mozart inside the cabin takes away from the time I could be spending learning to hear the natural music that goes on continually, without batteries, outside the cabin.

Will it always be this way? Can I find some kind of balance between both worlds, or will I have to choose one over the other? I don't know yet. Maybe it's too early to tell. Ten years for eight small pines. How long to change the landscape of one human heart? I wait on the middle ground to see what happens next.

NON-LAWN

When I first realized I had to live somewhere quiet and empty or go insane like those over-sensitive siblings in *The Fall of the House of Usher* who were driven mad by the acuteness of their own senses, I tried to think how I could possibly manage it. Work made me crazy, too, so I'd never be able to earn enough money to afford a cozy little coastal cottage or some gingerbread chalet in the mountains. The best I could do, I thought, would be to buy a single acre somewhere, the cheapest acre of land ever sold. Then I would build a house directly in the center of the land and plant hundreds of trees around it so that, eventually, I'd be protected from the noise and rude invasiveness of other humans.

The hardest part about this, I knew, would be the lawn. If my acre had to be anywhere in a civilized area, my neighbors would probably object to living next to what looked like an abandoned Christmas tree farm gone up to seed. They would want a lawn and a sidewalk nicely bordered with flowers. But I knew I wouldn't have time for lawns and flowers. All my time would be spent either earning the money to pay for my acre or enjoying it. Besides, I am a hunter-gatherer, not a farmer. It would defeat the purpose of living on my own place if I had to waste valuable time fertilizing and mowing and planting and weeding and participating in that cruel American tradition of keeping up with the Joneses.

Then the inspiration hit that I could inflict myself on my own family. After all, they had all kinds of land, much more than a single acre, and if I was even remotely nice to them, they would probably let me stay. So I moved here. And on the Gulch, one of the very best parts is the lawn. My yard consists of about an acre of armpit high grass and weeds that gets mowed, once a year, for hay. My neighbors, the cows (whom I have no trouble keeping up with), also come by occasionally and do a bit of trimming and leave slowly solidifying units of fertilizer. Once in a while I hack off hunks of grass that get in my way. I try to pull the beggar's lice because it's easier to do that than pick those things out of my socks. But mostly I enjoy whatever I happen to get—dandelions, bull thistles, skunk cabbage, Indian tobacco, wild roses, Syringa, blue bells, bachelor buttons, and a great waving ocean of grass.

It's perfect. An acre of grass. Five hundred acres of trees. Me. Throughout the year I subscribe to the theories of my human mentor, that laziest of men, Henry David Thoreau. He especially loved to watch his neighbors do all the backbreaking work of keeping up their homesteads. Then he would stroll by, enjoying the flowers and the tidy landscaping, taking the best part, the view, that his neighbors rarely had time to see. I confess to doing this when I leave here, amazed at the perfection of other yards, stunned that I can enjoy that beauty for free and then go home and spread a blanket in my patch of weeds to read books and take naps all summer long.

I wonder what would happen if the rest of America ever found out about the joys of the non-lawn. Would they cling to the civilized tradition of the lawn, devoting their brief weekends to the god of perfect grass, or would there be a revolution from

coast to coast, with lot-sized nature preserves springing up everywhere? I don't know. I guess I don't care. I've already found my paradise.

AIR

My family has this myth that we are related, probably illegitimately, to Benjamin Franklin. Although we have a history of inventing odd little gadgets and a fondness for kite flying, I never really believed there was a connection. But recently I saw an old movie, and in it, the portly Benjamin Franklin was stretched out in an armchair, buck naked, wafting the air from two open windows over his body in graceful, circular movements. Franklin was a great believer in air baths.

For the first time, I felt a bit of kinship. The air. To be out in the air. I have felt the need to be in the air all my life.

In my first real job I was a paper shuffler for a stock broker-age in Seattle. Every afternoon we had to take the old printout of accounts up the street to an adjacent building to be shredded. The other women in my department hated this job, hated having to go outside in the rain, getting wet, messing up their hair. But I volunteered. All afternoon I watched the clock until at last it was time to bundle up the dog-eared sheets and carry them outside. I hurried purposefully through the building until I reached the door, and then no person on this earth could have walked more slowly. I stepped into the air and lifted my face to the sun or the rain. I stood. I stretched. I looked around. As the slow cars lumbered up the street, I breathed in the carbon-monoxide air as if it were an elixir. I crept up the steep sidewalk and then back down again, small steps, stretching my time of freedom. Inside the office there was only recirculated air and drudgery and the little death of the 8:00 to 5:00, but outside was air and sky and freedom and life.

"Whew," I would say when I finally returned, sliding back behind my desk. "Long line for the shredder today."

I think they believed me. I think it would never have occurred to my fellow workers that I lived for those ten minutes every day when I could go outside.

Now I go outside all the time and all the kinds of air are like vintages of wine. There is the morning air when the whole world smells dewy and ready to begin again. There is the air of summer, so hot and dry it feels like it could float away from the earth. In August, the air smells of baking bread as the wheat ripens in fields for miles around. There is the incredible air of wet earth after a long-awaited rain. There is the air so saturated with pine it makes me dizzy. There is the air in winter, so pure and cold it freezes the hairs in my nostrils and burns its way into my lungs. In early spring, there is that first moment when the ground begins to thaw and I can smell the earth again. There is the air in March or April that lets me take my coat off for the first time. I can still feel winter against my bare arms and yet it is so wonderful to be able to move unencumbered, a slim shadow of my usually bundled self. There is the air that rises up from the spring as I crouch to fill the water jugs, cool and damp and thick with the smell of the life clustered around that trickling oasis.

In summer I lift out the three windows of the cabin and open the door wide, and then all the air of the earth can flow through the screens. I turn my world inside out, and invite the outside in.

Just now I'm reading one of those women's books that tells us we should accept our bodies and be proud of them. It's August, very hot, still over 90° at 5:30 p.m. I spent most of the day barefoot, wearing shorts and a wet T-shirt. But now I need water. I put my shoes on. I get the T-shirt wet again, but I'm tired of that clammy sensation against my skin, of feeling moldy and yet still hot. So I take the shirt back off and put it aside. However, this only serves to make me more aware of my bra, an awful contraption of synthetics and elastic hot against my skin. I take it off, too.

I peer carefully through all the windows. There is one combine working way off over the canyon. I can't hear the noise of any other machines. They've already harvested the peas in the north field. The barley in the west field isn't ready yet. Too early in the year for hunters. It seems unlikely that anyone is going to see me. I get a dry T-shirt, just in case. Am I really going to do this? Yes. I came here to experience things. I can't have adventures unless I'm willing to participate. So I grab two jugs and the water carrying stick and step outside.

The hot dry air touches me in places that have never been touched before. I spread my arms. The air bathes me, warm rather than hot, the light breeze cooling against my skin. I walk slowly up to the spring. So this is how men feel most of the summer, T-shirts off in two quick tugs and then wadded up to hang from a hip pocket.

I feel liberated. I feel sensuous and aware, walking up the trail bare chested, my breasts bobbing happily, freed from their usual restraints. My skin tingles, alive in a way it's never been alive before. Part of it is fear. What if someone does see me? Part of it is discovery. Why have I waited so long to try this? I feel open to the earth. It seems a good thing to be wearing my own skin, my animal skin, instead of the manufactured coverings of the civilized world.

As I crouch to fill the first jug, I see my breasts reflected in the water. They look nice floating there. They look beautiful, a part of me, nothing to be covered up as though I am ashamed. Later, I stand, the sun warm on my bare back. The air seems to pull close around me, silken against every pore of my body. I breathe in air as a fish breathes in water. The atmosphere has become my ocean and I would like to swim in it always. I cup my hands, filling them with the vibrant air, and lift them high over my head. I think of Benjamin Franklin and know that in this one thing, at least, we are kin.

WORSHIP

I stand facing the east. In my right hand is the sacred vessel. In my left hand is the sacred stopper. I stretch my arms wide and wave both objects in fundamentalist, Halleluiah praise just as the sun, looking for these few moments like the fire it is made of, appears between the far off trees.

It occurs to me that I repeat this ritual every morning. It is this moment when I first see the sun, more than any other action, that marks the beginning of my day. What I'm actually doing is shaking the rinse water out of the chamber pot and the chamber pot lid before I set them out to air. But because I tend to set my schedule by the sun year round, this practical activity and the rising of the sun often coincide. Anthropologists, studying me, could easily take this for a religious rite.

And perhaps it is a religious rite. I did not come here seeking religion. Instead, religion has sought me. Like everything else, it began slowly. Loneliness gave way to acceptance gave way to an awareness that I am not alone. There is a presence here. Perhaps it is the animal life, all the secretive creatures who make their homes around me. I see them just often enough to remind me that I am not the only life form in my universe. Maybe the presence I feel is that, the simple life force of all the growing things, rocks and trees and insects and animals and birds. Or maybe it is my own soul spread large to fill the empty spaces.

I have tried to name it God. I have tried to name it Goddess. But this presence feels bigger than any name. And it feels androgynous—not male, not female, but something beyond either male or female. It's not a name in my mind, but a sensitivity I feel to its presence, an opening to its power. I can be a part of it; it dwells inside of me.

I have tried to make this presence into a conventional religion, but it seems too big for a conventional religion. It could never be confined within a building. Also, traditional religions seem too tied up with humans, especially, for the most part, with various human fanatics, male gender, from the Middle East. Their rituals seem tainted with too many layers of human error. But this presence I feel is beyond the human. Humans are but a small part of its domain.

Many people, though, seem to want this human intervention. They are relieved to lose themselves in the bureaucracy and rules and social aspects of "real" religions so they don't have to actually confront that elemental force of the supernatural. They want spirituality with seat belts. Others use the familiar ceremonies to help them reach the metaphysical. They need the focusing power of litanies and candlelight to help lift them into the sublime. But I, in my brazen pride, get impatient with intermediaries. I want to be the shaman. Not trusting other people's interpretations of whatever it is that we call "god," I want to go directly to the source. And somehow that source is available to me here.

What can it be? Manifestation of my own needs? Bits and pieces of all my old beliefs? Catholicism with a woman pope. The "Force" envisioned by George Lucas. Pantheism. God in nature. The power of living things. The animism of Native Americans who see life in everything around them. Mysticism. Yin and

Yang. I don't know. It is a presence. I feel it. I believe.

This presence is all-present. At the most unexpected moments, I am suddenly aware of its approach and I am transported into its sphere. In the real world, the spiritual slips away too easily. An hour on Sunday or the Sabbath, and it is gone, too ephemeral to combat the distractions of modern life. But here, unless I stubbornly close myself off, the spiritual envelops me. Everything I do becomes religious. I feel the connection in the smallest actions—the play of light on a spoon as I sit down at the desk to have breakfast, a pause when I'm stacking wood to watch the feral clouds rush across the sky, the smooth way my bones move inside my flesh as I walk up the hill to experience that quietest moment just as the sun sets and the whole planet holds its breath.

Little things, all day long, uplift me. The big things leave me stunned. I hear the unmistakable honking and step out onto the ramp and in moments, the "V" of Canadian geese is directly overhead, seemingly inches above me. I hear the beating of their wings and feel the downdraft of air. I vibrate like a sympathetic string to the combined power of their labored quest. For long minutes after they are out of sight to the south, I stand, shaken. This is awe. This is wonder. This is something beyond the everyday world.

The moon is full. The November ground is covered with snow. The air is crystal. There is no wind. I walk out into the field beyond the house to bask in the silvery light. I feel the sheen of the moon enter my soul and brighten the dark places there. I turn slowly. I breathe quickly. And suddenly, without any warning, it is all around me, the presence. It is huge, filling the entire draw, extending up toward the sky. And it is laughing. I feel its proximity in waves of laughter, in bawdy, boisterous, uncontrollable joy. It is huge and powerful and enjoying itself immensely. I sink to my knees in the snow and it encompasses me for a moment. I feel a great bubbling lightness enter me. And then I am weeping because it is too big, too overwhelming, too joyous to bear. Yet I want to bear it. But even as I call out for it to stay, it is moving on, gone in a whoosh of air, flowing over the earth, off to touch other souls.

I stay on my knees. My heartbeat slows. I blink. Finally, I get up. I stand for a long time in the moonlight. There are no words for what has just happened, but I do believe.

WIND III

I t has been eight months since the night of the big wind. I can no longer remember quite so clearly the shapes of the trees that used to be here. I've stopped trying to superimpose those remembered silhouettes onto the new skyline.

For a long time, the needles clung to the three surviving limbs on the big, straight pine. Gradually they faded and then turned a bright orangey-brown. It hurt to see the needles fight to stay alive and then, losing that battle, to shriek out their agony for months in such a lurid, unnatural color. Now the needles have all fallen off and the three bare branches don't stand out quite so noticeably against the living trees. The elephant tree, all character gone, a featureless stump, is being dwarfed by the trees around it. The remaining bottom half of the tree that used to arch across the creek is still there as I look out through the window, and the needles on the branches are still green, although I worry that it, too, will die.

Meanwhile, nature and I have reached a cease-fire. I accept now that there can be no safe place while I live on this earth. I accept that pain will find me no matter how hard I try to hide from it. It feels like a betrayal of my old idealistic standards and yet grown-up to finally admit that life can never be perfect. For years I believed that there was one special place and one special way of living that would weave a magical protection around me. I was sure I had found that place in Dead Cow Gulch. Now I know that even though the Gulch is more wonderful than any place I've ever lived before, it, too, will sometimes betray me. I know that if I'm really going to live, I have to accept all the parts of life that come to me. I have to embrace the winter windstorms as well as the summer miracles. Some days the potential bleakness of the time that stretches ahead of me makes me weak with despair. Other days it seems like I am only truly human and alive when I accept the present pain and decide to go on in spite of it.

Life is danger. Life is change. I ride the wave as best I can.

GATES

During the summer, I share the canyon with about fifty head of cattle. This means that the canyon is fenced. Theoretically, the cows have no way out. Theoretically, humans do.

In Idaho, we use barbed wire gates which are sort of movable extensions of the barbed wire fences. Usually there are three or four vertical poles strung with two strands of wire. The human simply stretches this contraption across the opening, holds it upright, and secures it in place with a wire loop, also barbed, attached to the planted fence post. In theory, this method sounds simple and straightforward. In practice, it sucks.

For men, with all that natural upper body strength, it is fairly easy to jerk the gate upright, wrestle the gate pole in close with one hand, and bring the loop down over it with the other. Because the gates must be pulled very tight to discourage bovine adventurists, most gates are equipped with a lever of wood or iron that dangles from a strand of barbed wire. Even men sometimes use this lever, bracing it against the gate pole and pushing on it with all their strength to inch the pole close enough to be captured with the loop.

For less muscular humans, using these gates is not quite so simple. Even opening them is hard, trying to get that tight, barbed loop up and off the rough-textured pole. The moment the gate is freed, it vaults away like an arrow released from a bow to land in a tangled heap of wire and poles. Disentangling it so it can be closed again, making sure the strands of wire aren't twisted, takes strength and patience, and usually involves getting impaled several times. Once upright, the gate is heavy with an almost sentient determination to lie back down again. Using both hands and my upper body, I try to get the gate close enough to hook the gate pole into the bottom loop of wire. This accomplished, I realize that the gate pole is still four feet away from the top loop. Using both hands and my upper body, I struggle to get the pole closer. Finally, I'm able to reach the dangling lever, cutting myself several more times on the wire that holds it. Usually it's hanging on the wrong side from the previous struggle and has to be shifted around so the central part of the lever contacts the pole, creating the exact balance needed to make the lever work. Meanwhile, I cling desperately to the gate pole one-handed, praying not to lose the ground I've gained so far in getting the pole this close. If I'm lucky, I'm able to throw the lever across the top wire of the gate and hold it there while the pole is still within reach. Now comes the work of levering the pole closer still, praying that the lever doesn't slip, sending the gate twanging back into the original tangled heap. Once the pole is within reach of the loop, I keep the lever in position with my chest and use both hands to try to get the loop down over the pole. There. Simple and easy. I'm sweating and exhausted, ripped and torn, but the gate is closed.

My real solution to this ridiculous system would be nice wooden gates on hinges with secure latches. A partial solution would be to use plain rather than barbed wire for the loop and for the tether that holds the lever. My temporary solution for the three or four times each day I go up and back from the spring, has been to tie a piece of baling twine to the upright post and the gate pole, leaving just a little slack. Then, when I lift the loop to open the gate, at least the gate doesn't recoil, but is held upright by the baling twine. I pick the spot where the wire sags lowest and carefully step over. Then I lever the pole back into position and pull the loop down over it. The first time I tried the twine and didn't have to go through the steps of gate untangling and gate uprighting, I felt as though I had triumphed over a hundred years of brutish stupidity. My solution was far from perfect, but at least it circumvented parts of the usual ordeal.

The gates make me think about men, those mysterious creatures I have tried for so long to figure out. I wonder if it is their strength alone that makes them act the way they do.

Sometimes I help my brothers with haying. It is a killer job. It's usually July—dry and roasting in Idaho. The bales are huge and scratchy. The beds of the trucks we have to buck the bales up to seem impossibly high. The metal barn where we stack the bales is like a bake oven. I seldom last more than half a day. I'm wet with sweat, all body salts depleted. My arms feel like they're going to fall off. My eyes and throat are scratchy from the constant cloud of alfalfa dust and pollen we work in. My back aches. I try to use the traditional, practiced motion of boosting the bale up onto the truck with a perfectly timed, lifted knee, but my muscles soon give out. My brothers and the other men on the hay crew look exhausted, too, but somehow they keep going, all through the hot afternoon and on into the next day and the next.

How do they do that? Is it really easier for them because they're taller and because they have more upper body strength? Or have they just been trained from a very early age to endure more physical pain than I can even imagine?

I think of how women would do these things. Everything would be smaller. We might not dream of owning fifty cattle at once. Two or three would seem like plenty. We might domesticate the cattle more completely so that, stupid as cows can often be, they wouldn't need such barbarous fences to keep them in. If we had to make hay, the bales would be smaller. We'd do a hundred extra smaller lifts, rather than endure those fewer but heavier hoists that threaten to rip our guts out. The truck bed would be lower. We would rest more often and drink more water. It wouldn't be that important to us to compete with each other, pushing ourselves past the point of exhaustion. Haying would still be hard, hard work, but bearable. Nicer.

It's hard to say. If women ran the world, perhaps we, too, would want everything to be bigger and faster and more efficient. Gardening, once done with shovels and hoes, would become farming that has to be done with big machines, Caterpillar Challenger 65's and 1670 International Harvester combines with 1010 headers. Our compulsion for nesting, making things nice, pleasant, comfortable, inviting, might give way before the harsher necessities of global management.

Another gate up ahead. I stop my gender ruminations to tackle the present problem. Men are men and a mystery. Women are women and a mystery. I suppose that's what makes life so intriguing, this constant suspense, wondering if we'll ever figure each other out, wondering if we really want to. The gates stand between us, marking the differences and the divisions. Who will be the first to take them down?

PINHEAD

ou know those poignant stories that appear every other month or so in the *Reader's Digest* about the death of a beloved pet. (The pet is always a dog. No one ever seems to write about a beloved cat.) They're the kind of stories you cry over every time, even though you're determined not to. Well, the time has come for me to write one of those kinds of stories.

His name was Pinhead. Not very flattering, perhaps, but honest. Pinhead traveled everywhere with me, from "C" Street in Moscow to the student slums of Syracuse and back again, this time out to Dead Cow Gulch. He was small, quiet, cuddly, didn't cost a lot to keep. And like all best beloved acquaintances he was eccentric, quirky, and full of personality. Pinhead was my first computer.

Yesterday I received word that my new computer, a Macintosh Classic, is in. I'll pick it up on Monday. But Pinhead doesn't know about the Classic yet. As I sit here writing this, he is unaware that he is about to be replaced. How could he suspect anything? We've been together for so long.

It was February of 1984. Just when I'd finally saved up enough money to buy an IBM Selectric typewriter, the dream of half a lifetime, typewriters had become obsolete. So I was going to buy an IBM-PC, that solid, business-like, Big Blue machine. But then suddenly all the computer magazines I'd been buying started talking about Apple's new Macintosh. It was love at first sight. The Mac was gently rounded. It was cute. It looked approachable. It had a personality. It made me think lovingly of my 1977 Volkswagen Bug, the one I bought in a near panic that last year that Volkswagen still made Bugs. I loved the whole idea of the Macintosh. I loved its outsider, rebel status. I loved its user friendly interface.

So on March 26, 1984, I took Pinhead home. I decided right away that he was male because I was going through a period when I liked to imagine that males could be subservient to me. Pinhead had 128K of RAM, and a 400K disk drive. Just one. And a mouse.

Everything about Pinhead was delightful. That smiling face icon and the "Welcome to Macintosh" screen every time I started him up. The little song of the disk drive. The pictures in the scrapbook. The puzzle under the Apple menu. The trash can. WYSIWYG—what you see is what you get. Using the mouse to go exactly where I wanted to go in a document instead of the endless DOS machine routine—down arrow key, down arrow key, down arrow key, down arrow key . . . oops . . . up arrow key, right arrow key, right arrow key, right arrow key, etc., etc. etc. No DOS, for that matter. No function keys to memorize. No Control-Shift-hyphen-4 to get underlining.

Pinhead wrote several novels. He did lesson plans. He made birthday cards. He formatted scholarly papers. He put up with all the inconveniences of my nomadic existence. One apartment was so old it didn't even have a three-hole outlet, but Pinhead handled my jury-rigged adapter. I've lugged him through airports of all kinds, even in these later times, when we have to painfully prove that Pinhead is really a computer and not a bomb, enduring the sidelong, condescending glances of laptop computer users as they move briskly through the inspection while we struggle with power cords and disk insertion.

The cabin has been especially stressful for Pinhead. I strapped him to my packframe and hauled him out here. For the whole first week he just sat on the desk, wide-eyed, unable to believe that he was really expected to perform in this wilderness. He was startled by the noisy power of the generator, but eventually took to it. Then he had to make the switch to solar power, trusting the sun and the batteries and the inverter to keep him going. "Save every fifteen minutes," became an absolute rule. Pinhead doesn't have a fan. On hot days, I baby him along and he struggles to keep cranking. Cold days are tough, too. If I don't get the cabin warm enough first, his disk drive voice is baritone and even the usually fast operations are slow.

But time and rough living are beginning to take their toll. First, he got ridicule. Pinhead is not his original name. It was given to him by my fellow Mac hackers with their 2 megs of RAM and 40 meg hard disks and 68030 processors. They cup their hands disdainfully around Pinhead's "pregnant mouse," the quaintly clunky version that can't help looking outdated. Even a 512K brain transplant and the purchase of a second disk drive still left Pinhead miles behind his progeny. And it didn't help when I went through the Smithsonian's "Information Age" exhibit in 1990. I was chuckling at the funny looking, ancient computers and suddenly I was face to face with a 128K Mac just like Pinhead, an example of "early" breakthroughs in personal computing. My computer was a museum piece. What could possibly be older than that?

I should have realized he was getting on in years. The winter before I'd even seen the exhibit, I thought he was a goner. The screen had this bad habit of suddenly going black in the middle of a chapter. If I tapped Pinhead lightly on the side, I could usually get the screen to come back, but sometimes I had to shut down by Braille and try again the next day. Fortunately, a new power supply was all he needed, and he perked right up again. Then last month his external disk drive wore out. I was back to the constant in-out, in-out of a single drive machine. Almost $200.00 to fix it. Do I try to hold onto Pinhead, or accept that his long and useful life is over?

Technological greed won out over loyalty. I want a real word processing program, a spell checker, address data base, a spreadsheet, all the Cliff Johnson games and Steve Halls' Moose program. I lust after the speed and convenience of a hard drive.

And yet I will miss Pinhead so much. No new computer, even my new Macintosh, will have the spunk, the big-hearted generosity, the sense of adventure that Pinhead had. It may be years before the Classic gets that stained place on top, the place where I kissed Pinhead over and over, delighted with the way he slaved tirelessly with me and made my work so much easier and more creative and more fun.

Pinhead is going now to a new home. They're going to fix his disk drive and use him for word processing. He'll have real WWP electricity and central heating. Hopefully, he'll have long quiet spells between school papers to dream his 1,0,1,1,0 dreams. Maybe sometimes he'll remember my touch on his keyboard, and the wild, adventurous part of his life when we wrote wonderful novels together and sang our computer/human song. Good-bye, Pinhead. You've been my truest friend.

CROWS

I like crows. Crows are the Danny DeVitos of the bird world. While all the other birds flit secretively about, feathers often so mottled and camouflaged it's hard to spot them, the crows are starkly and unrepentantly black. On the coldest, bleakest days when the yellow jackets, once weightless blurs of speed, lumber across the floor heavy as cows, when it seems like all living creatures have hunkered down out of sight, when I haven't seen anyone but me for days, the crows will come flapping into view, sharp punctuation against the grey sky.

They're unfocused fliers. Sometimes they obviously have places to go and make good progress across the sky. But often they wander rather aimlessly and forget to flap and then have to make herculean efforts to get themselves airborne again. Hawks seem to soar forever on the thermals above the canyon, only a smooth wingstroke now and then needed to keep them circling. Crows have to work harder. There is a lot of clumsy flapping and complaining when they fly. They are like the people who stand at the back of the aerobics class, trying to get with the program and yet dragging their feet all the way.

The crows are great curmudgeons. They're not shy about getting things off their chest. Their voices, the sound of a chain-smoking bass-baritone with a lousy cold gargling Listerine, are

116

the voices for which the word "raucous" was invented. I usually hear them, long before I see them, kvetching their way into view. It's cold. I'm hungry. My wings hurt. There's nothing out here to eat. They labor across the sky, and I laugh at them, and they probably complain about that, too.

I like the crows. They see past the pretense of polite civility and say what they mean. The crows are survivors. They hang around when everyone else has given up. They're a solid, comical, crabby presence all year round and I treasure their company. Dead Cow Gulch wouldn't be the same without them.

ALONE

It is the Stockholm syndrome. Loneliness, once the captor of my spirit, now seems like a dear companion and wears the gentler name of solitude. It happened slowly, gradually. Instead of fighting loneliness, I learned to take it inside of me and to fill it with thoughts and fantasies and plans. I structured it to be productive. I learned to count on its solid presence. It seems like I am never lonely anymore.

Perhaps there is a reason. Things have changed since my initial victory over or acceptance of aloneness. I remember how one of my friends, of good New England Puritan stock, used to yell out to hitchhikers she passed, "Get a job! Buy a car!" Regretfully, I have followed her advice. After 1983, that first tough year of scraping by at Dead Cow Gulch, before I returned again, I got a job. I bought a car. Had to. Mind you, it's the smallest possible job I could get. I have weekends and summers off. But still, it is a job. My life has gotten more complicated. I know people now, and they find ways to lure me out of my solitude. It's been a long time since I've had the luxury of spending one of those ten-day periods out here where I forget the shapings of human speech. Maybe I haven't really conquered loneliness at all. Maybe I just think I have because I rarely get to experience it anymore.

It's hard to say. Despite the job, I have far more solitude than

I ever had in the real "real world," and yet I would gladly take on even more. It's most noticeable in the excitement I feel every time I'm able to come out here. The packing up seems to take forever. What will I forget this time? Glasses? Mayonnaise? Socks? Do I have all the things I need to make these five rare solitary days perfect?

When I do arrive, there is a flurry of activity. I have to touch things and see what's changed and build a fire and unpack and haul water and get everything functioning again. Then, often, there is an empty space. I feel alien here. I can't remember the rhythm. I don't know what to do. Shrouded in the rush and stimulation of the social whirl, I feel defensive about giving up that protection.

Soon, though, it all comes back to me. I think those first long, lonely stretches of time out here formed a foundation. I'm like a subject who's frequently been hypnotized. I've fallen under the spell of Dead Cow Gulch so often before, that now I know the route. The sight of the bushy, double-crowned pine at the top of the hill or a few quiet moments at my desk or a brief walk out to stare at the pond and I am entranced, back under. Alone. To be alone. To be free from all desires save my own.

Sometimes I worry that it is only selfishness. My friends are so committed to their work. They're so involved with so many things. They visit each other and go to meetings together and help each other out. I find myself constantly saying no. Even though I'm tempted by the thought of a leisurely dinner in town or an evening spent at a lecture or one of those late into the night philosophical conversations, something else pulls at me, Dead Cow Gulch, time alone, selfish pleasures, the ritualistic calming of solitaire by candlelight.

I tend now to depend on quick hits of friendship and socializing. A good talk with my office mate. A lunch packed full of conversation about important things. An hour at a party, that's plenty, making the rounds, touching bases. But beyond that point, everything becomes too loud, too rushed, too manic with alcohol and high spirits, and I feel myself turning inward for escape. A vision grows in my mind—a small cabin, still and waiting in the moonlight—and I long to be there where once again I can hear myself think.

My friends are wonderfully tolerant. They seem to accept this need of mine, the anxious plotting that begins at the outset of any social event when I'm already trying to figure out just how quickly I can get away. I do better with my letter friends, the people I've written to for years and years. We never see each other, and yet we connect. I read their letters over and over and that is enough to keep me part of the human race. I depend, too, on family. They have that genetic closeness that doesn't require the time-consuming maintenance of friendship. I see them, we smile, I help them, they help me, we part easily to go back to our separate lives. They are patient, too, used to my furtive comings and goings, the way I bolt from situations that are too loud, too much.

I have this fantasy that someday I can do both—social and solitude. But in the quintet of the necessities that shape my existence—living, writing, survival, work, and social—social always loses. I refuse to not live, to give up consciousness and all the little pleasures that enrich my life. I must write. I cannot not write. The labor of survival, from patching the roof to paying the health insurance bill, is inescapable. Work, then, seems like the obvious element to dispense with, but so far work is too closely tied to survival to be eliminated. Social loses every time.

Meanwhile, until I can quit my day job and devote the resulting free time to socializing, I watch for signs of pathological reclusiveness. But so far my craving for solitude seems like a healthy thing. I come here with such joy. The days are full of wonder. I read and think and learn so much. The longer I stay, the better I feel, as I'm pulled deeper and deeper into the dream of the canyon. For me, somehow, this solitary state is natural. It's where I truly live. It's where I want to stay.

TO BE

I want to live in the state of the verb "to be." I just want to exist, to be, to experience, to observe. But I am stuck in a world that lives in the state of the verb "to do." We are what we eat. We are what we do. We must work hard to make money so that we can spend money so that we can keep the economy going. Left to our own devices, we would be slovenly dolts, but driven by our culture, we rush around and fill every moment of the day and buy time-saving gadgets so we can accomplish even more.

"Bored. I would get so bored if I didn't work." That's what people tell me. I love bored. I live for bored. Being bored would mean that I had read every book I ever wanted to read and taken every class and traveled to every country and explored every inch of the canyon and achieved all my goals and learned to play the bagpipes besides. Only then would I have time to be bored.

But even then I wouldn't really be bored because when you finally have absolutely nothing else left to do, that's when you finally get to be. In the state of the verb "to be" it's okay to plop down on the ground and get lost in the ballet of moving clouds overhead. It's okay to waste an extra hour in bed, not sleeping, but just drifting in and out of consciousness. It's okay to spend a morning really looking at a tree, studying all its colors, the texture of its bark, the powerful surge of it against your body when it sways in the wind.

It took me a long time to figure this out, that the reason I could never fit comfortably in the world was because I was living in an incompatible verb state. I do the "to do" verb most of the time, too much, lately, in fact. And doing is good. It keeps me grounded, keeps me from becoming a creature of pure daydream with no ties left to reality. The secret is balance. Everyone knows how to do "to do." But most of us experience "to be" so rarely, we don't know how to be when we finally get there. "To be or not to be?" Hamlet knew the agony well and expressed it perfectly. The whirl of our world comes to a stop, and we panic, realizing that suddenly we have time to look at ourselves, to look at our lives, to experience introspection. So we quickly turn on the television or hurry out to go shopping, lest we be forced to see what we have become.

It's a lot of work just to be. You must overcome guilt and years of conditioning. You must face emotions like sadness and disappointment and confusion and despair. You must suddenly become accountable for your life. Instead of mindlessly letting life slip through your fingers, you must grab hold and husband the time you have and make it mean something.

Oh, but it's worth it. I still turn unconscious. I still let the fast pace of life blur the details. But when I can make myself stop and when I can let myself be, the richness of it is beyond words. I hug myself, not believing my luck, that I can live in a world of such beauty and fascination. I stop. I hold still. I open my eyes. I travel to that unique mental place where it is possible and acceptable to live in the state of the verb "to be."

MELT

I wake up with the roaring sound still in my ears. It rained hard most of the night, the familiar drumming on the woodshed roof and the shed's tin roof and the skylight just over my head. I snuggled down in my blankets, happy to be dry, thinking of what a slushy mess this early rain was going to make with all that snow out there. But when the rain stopped around 4:00 a.m., this deeper sound became audible and it filled my dreams. It could be the wind because the wind is blowing, but it doesn't sound like the wind.

Anxious to find an answer to this riddle, I climb down and strain to see through the windows, but it's not light yet and I can't tell if the trees are moving or not. It's cold, March cold, and yet not as cold as usual. I go into my morning routine in a muddled way, confused by this new sound I still can't identify.

As soon as it gets light enough, I abandon the ordinary sequence to hurry outside. All the snow is gone, all of it. The white world I went to bed in is suddenly brown. Trees glisten and shake themselves as if unaccustomed to raising their branches without the frozen weight of snow. The roar out here is much louder. And there's something in the pond, a big, shaggy, tawny brown hump. What on earth! I move forward, impeded by thick mud. The road is gone. In its place is a bank of mud with three or four brisk streams moving through it, all of them plunging into the pond. Instead of the single feeder creek above, the pond now has half a dozen random waterways flowing into it. Even more astonishing, the pond suddenly has an island, a big mud island planted with golden stubble washed down from the west field.

The pond is overflowing. Sheets of water ignore the normal outlet drain that is no longer adequate and flow over the top, moving in a disorganized tangle of streams to the creek below. The creek is full, rushing along between the narrow, steep banks, black with mud. I step over the land bridge carefully, remembering the fate of dead cows, and follow the creek down its far side. There are rapids and waterfalls and deep subterranean clefts that turn the roar of water into a low-voiced rumble.

I go back and forth between the pond and the creek for over an hour. It has stopped raining, but the flood of water shows no signs of abating. It washes down from the fields and runs in a stream down the road that leads to the spring and pours through the creek above the pond. The pond itself fills and overflows again and again, sending more water into the creek below which tumbles on down into the canyon.

Well. Chinooks, they call them, sudden warm winds from the direction of the Indian lands that turn winter to spring overnight. The unexpected rise in temperature and the heavy rain have combined to set the whole world in motion. I stop long enough for breakfast, but then I'm outside again. I recognize the roar of my own creek now, but there is still a deeper, more powerful sound I can't figure out. I go for the high ground, following the perimeter of the alfalfa field until I reach the topmost point. I catch sight of something moving way down in the canyon, something brown and huge.

Suddenly I realize that it's the river, the Middle Potlatch, turned into a wide brown snake coiling fiercely along the canyon floor. I've never been able to see the river from here before. Usually, it's little bigger than my own creek, a thin trickle of water over dry stones. When I do stand here and look down, I imagine where the river is because I'm familiar with the contours of the land where it flows. But this morning it is visible, a real river, brown and rushing, full of power. The canyon walls act like a giant soundboard and send the roar of it echoing around me.

As I walk slowly back to the cabin, my genetic farmer instincts surface and I know that this early melt is too soon, too fast. The erosion, that instant island in the pond, will be terrible. But my spirit refuses to join these realistic thoughts. I walk in a world suddenly released. All that was frozen still is now rushing and roaring along with precipitate power. The air, frozen dry for so long, has moisture in it. The land, frozen hard, is coming back to life. I can smell pine needles and rotting leaves and mud and damp bark. I feel the river flowing inside of me, a pent-up release, a headlong rushing toward tomorrow.

They call it spring, but a better name would be melt. It is here. Melt is here. After all this time, I know the cycle of the seasons. It will snow again and get icy cold and try to lock us all back into the peaceful somnolence of winter, but we know now that spring is coming. The river, the trees, the coyotes, the seeds of tiny wildflowers, the blades of grass and the one, lone human, we all know that the wheel is turning again. We are awake. Each new day will be longer than the one before. Each drop of rain will touch the earth with life. Soon we will be into that golden time of the year with long days and exuberant growth and warmth soaking in deep.

Winter is good. I've learned to survive it well, to experience its quiet joys, but the seasons coming up—spring, summer, fall —melt, growth, harvest—those are the months I live for. That is what I love. I go back into the cabin and close the door. This time the sound doesn't diminish. The roar continues on in my head. My mind fills with possibilities. Time to begin another year of life here on Dead Cow Gulch.

95	**DATE DUE**
p Timmerman	
A Moore	
M. Carter	
TILLEY	
B Skold	
G Thomason	
01	
L Carson	
A Cheasebre	
02	
H Warden	
M Ryan	
M Vapovich	
J Woodke	